Learning IPython for Interactive Computing and Data Visualization

Learn IPython for interactive Python programming, high-performance numerical computing, and data visualization

Cyrille Rossant

[PACKT] open source*
PUBLISHING   community experience distilled

BIRMINGHAM - MUMBAI

Learning IPython for Interactive Computing and Data Visualization

First published: April 2013

Production Reference: 1150413

Published by Packt Publishing Ltd.
Livery Place
35 Livery Street
Birmingham B3 2PB, UK..

ISBN 978-1-78216-993-2

www.packtpub.com

Cover Image by Asher Wishkerman (wishkerman@hotmail.com)

Credits

Author
Cyrille Rossant

Reviewers
Francisco J. Blanco-Silva

Matthias Bussonnier

Acquisition Editor
Kartikey Pandey

Comissioning Editor
Maria D'souza

Sruthi Kutty

Technical Editors
Soumya Kanti

Veena Pagare

Copy Editor
Insiya Morbiwala

Alfida Paiva

Project Coordinator
Sneha Modi

Proofreader
Lauren Tobon

Indexer
Rekha Nair

Graphics
Aditi Gajjar

Ronak Shah

Production Coordinator
Nilesh R. Mohite

Cover Work
Nilesh R. Mohite

About the Author

Cyrille Rossant is a French researcher in quantitative neuroscience. A graduate of the Ecole Normale Supérieure, Paris, he holds a Master's degree and a Ph.D. in Mathematics and Computer Science. He uses IPython every day to model and simulate the brain and to analyze experimental data. He is the creator of a few scientific Python packages, including Playdoh (parallel computing) and Galry (high-performance interactive visualization).

I am grateful to the vibrant Python community for developing this great open platform for computational science. Devoting hard work to open-source software sometimes requires personal sacrifice, but it's worth the effort. In particular, I would like to thank Fernando Perez, creator of IPython, and all the development team for their awesome work on this library. Also, we regular Matplotlib users are all deeply grateful to its creator John Hunter, whose untimely passing in 2012 is a tragedy for the whole community and beyond.

I would also like to thank the reviewers for their helpful comments and suggestions. Finally, I am grateful to my family and Claire for their support during the writing of this book.

About the Reviewer

Matthias Bussonnier is a young French physicist working in biophysics. He has been a core developer of IPython since 2011.

> I'd like to thank all my family, colleagues, as well as the IPython core team for their help and the fun moments spent developing for the open source community.

Dr. Francisco J. Blanco-Silva, the owner of a scientific consulting company — Tizona Scientific Solutions — and adjunct faculty in the Department of Mathematics of the University of South Carolina has obtained his formal training as an applied mathematician at Purdue University. He enjoys problem solving, learning, and teaching. An avid programmer and blogger, when it comes to writing he relishes finding that common denominator among his passions and skills, and making it available to everyone.

He has written the technical book *Learning SciPy for Numerical and Scientific Computing, Packt Publishing.*

He has also co-authored Chapter 5 of the book *Modeling Nanoscale Imaging in Electron Microscopy, Springer 201, Thomas Vogt and Wolfgang Dahmen, Springer.*

www.PacktPub.com

Support files, eBooks, discount offers and more

You might want to visit www.PacktPub.com for support files and downloads related to your book.

Did you know that Packt offers eBook versions of every book published, with PDF and ePub files available? You can upgrade to the eBook version at www.PacktPub.com and as a print book customer, you are entitled to a discount on the eBook copy. Get in touch with us at service@packtpub.com for more details.

At www.PacktPub.com, you can also read a collection of free technical articles, sign up for a range of free newsletters and receive exclusive discounts and offers on Packt books and eBooks.

http://PacktLib.PacktPub.com

Do you need instant solutions to your IT questions? PacktLib is Packt's online digital book library. Here, you can access, read and search across Packt's entire library of books.

Why Subscribe?

- Fully searchable across every book published by Packt
- Copy and paste, print and bookmark content
- On demand and accessible via web browser

Free Access for Packt account holders

If you have an account with Packt at www.PacktPub.com, you can use this to access PacktLib today and view nine entirely free books. Simply use your login credentials for immediate access.

Table of Contents

Preface

You are a programmer using Python as a scripting language, maybe for software development. Learning IPython will let you use Python *interactively* in a highly efficient way, for example, when exploring algorithms or analyzing data. In addition, it is the best way to be introduced to the most advanced capabilities of the platform, namely numerical computing, interactive visualization, and parallel programming.

What this book covers

Chapter 1, *Getting Started with IPython*, is a short, hands-on introduction to the key features of IPython. It will give you a broad overview of what IPython offers. All features introduced in this chapter will be covered in the subsequent chapters.

Chapter 2, *Interactive Work with IPython*, will show you how to use Python interactively from the IPython command-line interface, and how the numerous *magic commands* will help you considerably improve your productivity. This chapter will also introduce you to the IPython notebook, a modern tool for reproducible and collaborative interactive programming.

Chapter 3, *Numerical Computing with IPython*, contains an introduction to the numerical computing features of Numpy and Pandas, which can be conveniently used from IPython. These tools are essential as soon as you need to analyze large amounts of data, or more generally when you need to perform efficient numerical computations.

Chapter 4, *Interactive Plotting and Graphical Interfaces*, covers the graphical capabilities of Matplotlib, and shows how they integrate smoothly in IPython. Matplotlib is a very powerful graphical library, which allows you to either generate high-quality figures or to visualize data interactively.

Chapter 5, High-Performance and Parallel Computing, is an advanced chapter detailing various ways by which you can accelerate your code, such as parallel computing and dynamic C compilation. The former method consists in distributing tasks across cores or computers, which is particularly easy to do with IPython. The latter method lets you write code in a superset of Python (using the Cython library), which is then dynamically compiled in C for dramatic speed improvements.

Chapter 6, Customizing IPython, shows you how you can customize IPython, create new magic commands, and use custom representations in the IPython notebook.

What you need for this book

This book assumes familiarity with the Python language. In addition, you will need to have a Python installation on your computer (Windows, OS X, or Linux). You will also need to install IPython as well as a few other external libraries. The installation procedures are detailed in *Chapter 1, Getting Started with IPython.*

Who this book is for

This book is intended for Python programmers who want to learn IPython for the advanced console, the notebook, and the interactive computing facilities offered by the platform. Students, hackers, scientists, and hobbyists who are interested in interactive computing, data analysis, and visualization will also be interested in this book, but will need to learn the basics of Python first. Fortunately, Python is a very accessible language, and a lot of books, courses, and tutorials are available.

Conventions

In this book, you will find a number of styles of text that distinguish between different kinds of information. Here are some examples of these styles, and an explanation of their meaning.

Code words in text are shown as follows: "For instance, the standard Unix commands pwd, ls, cd are available in IPython."

A block of code is set as follows:

```
print("Running script.")
x = 12
print("'x' is now equal to {0:d}.".format(x))
```

Any command-line input or output is written as follows:

```
In [1]: run script.py
Running script.
'x' is now equal to 12.
In [2]: x
Out[2]: 12
```

New terms and **important words** are shown in bold. Words that you see on the screen, in menus or dialog boxes for example, appear in the text like this: "Click on the **New Notebook** button at the top right of the page".

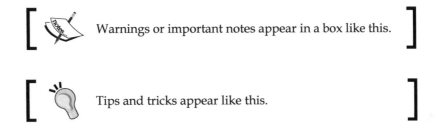

> Warnings or important notes appear in a box like this.

> Tips and tricks appear like this.

Reader feedback

Feedback from our readers is always welcome. Let us know what you think about this book—what you liked or may have disliked. Reader feedback is important for us to develop titles that you really get the most out of.

To send us general feedback, simply send an e-mail to feedback@packtpub.com, and mention the book title through the subject of your message.

If there is a topic that you have expertise in and you are interested in either writing or contributing to a book, see our author guide on www.packtpub.com/authors.

Customer support

Now that you are the proud owner of a Packt book, we have a number of things to help you to get the most from your purchase.

Downloading the example code

You can download the example code files for all Packt books you have purchased from your account at http://www.packtpub.com. If you purchased this book elsewhere, you can visit http://www.packtpub.com/support and register to have the files e-mailed directly to you. In addition, all examples can be downloaded from the author's website: http://ipython.rossant.net.

Errata

Although we have taken every care to ensure the accuracy of our content, mistakes do happen. If you find a mistake in one of our books—maybe a mistake in the text or the code—we would be grateful if you would report this to us. By doing so, you can save other readers from frustration and help us improve subsequent versions of this book. If you find any errata, please report them by visiting http://www.packtpub.com/support, selecting your book, clicking on the **errata submission form** link, and entering the details of your errata. Once your errata are verified, your submission will be accepted and the errata will be uploaded to our website, or added to any list of existing errata, under the Errata section of that title.

Piracy

Piracy of copyright material on the Internet is an ongoing problem across all media. At Packt, we take the protection of our copyright and licenses very seriously. If you come across any illegal copies of our works, in any form, on the Internet, please provide us with the location address or website name immediately so that we can pursue a remedy.

Please contact us at copyright@packtpub.com with a link to the suspected pirated material.

We appreciate your help in protecting our authors, and our ability to bring you valuable content.

Questions

You can contact us at questions@packtpub.com if you are having a problem with any aspect of the book, and we will do our best to address it.

Getting Started with IPython

1

In this chapter, we will first go through the IPython installation process and give an overview of the possibilities offered by IPython. IPython brings a highly improved Python console and the Notebook. In addition, it is an essential tool for interactive computing when it is combined with third-party specialized packages, such as NumPy and Matplotlib. These packages bring high-performance computing and interactive visualization facilities to the Python universe, with IPython being its cornerstone. At the end of this chapter, you will have IPython installed and the required packages on your computer, and you will have been through a short, hands-on overview of the most important features of IPython that we will detail in the subsequent chapters, such as:

- Running the IPython console
- Using IPython as a system shell
- Using the history
- Tab completion
- Executing a script with the `%run` command
- Quick benchmarking with the `%timeit` command
- Quick debugging with the `%pdb` command
- Interactive computing with Pylab
- Using the IPython Notebook
- Customizing IPython

Installing IPython and the recommended packages

In this section, we will see how you can install IPython and the other packages that we will be using in this book. For the most up-to-date information about the IPython installation, you should check the official website of IPython (http://ipython.org).

Prerequisites for IPython

First things first, what do you need to have on your computer before installing IPython? The good news is that IPython, and more generally all Python packages, can run, in principle, on most platforms (that is, Linux, Apple OS X, and Microsoft Windows). You also need to have a valid Python distribution installed on your system before installing and running IPython. The latest stable version of IPython at the time of writing is 0.13.1, and it officially requires Python 2.6, 2.7, 3.1, or 3.2.

Python 2.x and 3.x

The 3.x branch of Python is not backward compatible with the 2.x branch, which explains why the 2.7 version is still maintained. Even if most external Python packages used in this book are compatible with Python 3.x, some packages are still not compatible with this branch. At this time, the choice between Python 2.x and Python 3.x for a new project is typically dictated by the Python 3 support of the required external Python packages. The setups of the targeted users is also an important point to consider. In this book, we will use Python 2.7 and try to minimize the incompatibilities with Python 3.x. This issue is beyond the scope of this book, and we encourage you to search for information about how to write code for Python 2.x that is as compatible with Python 3.x as possible. This official web page is a good starting point:

http://wiki.python.org/moin/Python2orPython3

We will use Python 2.7 in this book. The 2.6 version is no longer maintained and, if you choose to stick with the 2.x branch, you should only use Python 2.7 as far as possible.

We will use other Python packages in this book that are typically used with IPython. These packages are mainly NumPy, SciPy, and Matplotlib, but there are additional packages we will use in some examples. Details about how to install them are provided in the next section *Installing an all-in-one distribution*.

There are several ways of installing IPython and the recommended packages. From the easiest to the hardest, you can do either of the following:

- Install a standalone, all-in-one Python distribution with a large variety of built-in Python packages
- Install separately only the packages you need

In the latter case, you can use binary installers or install the packages directly from the source code.

Installing an all-in-one distribution

This solution is by far the easiest. You can download a single binary installer that comes with a full Python distribution and a lot of widely used external packages, including IPython. Popular distributions include:

- The Enthought Python Distribution (EPD) and the new Canopy by Enthought:

  `http://www.enthought.com/`

- Anaconda by Continuum Analytics:

  `http://www.continuum.io/`

- Python(x,y), an open source project:

  `http://code.google.com/p/pythonxy/`

- ActivePython by ActiveState:

  `http://www.activestate.com/activepython`

All these distributions support Linux, OS X, and Windows, except Python(x,y) which only supports Windows. They all offer a free edition (and possibly a commercial edition) and they all contain IPython. ActivePython and EPD also ship with their own packaging systems; this makes it easy to install additional packages. These distributions contain most of the external packages we will be using in this book.

Installing the packages one by one

Sometimes you may prefer to install only the packages you need instead of installing a large all-in-one package. Fortunately, this should be straightforward on most recent systems. Binary installers are indeed available for Windows, OS X, and most common Linux distributions. Otherwise, there is always the possibility to install the packages from the source, which is generally easier than it sounds.

Packages websites

Here is a list of Python packages that we will mention in this book, along with their respective websites where you can find the most up-to-date information:

- IPython:

  `http://ipython.org`

- NumPy, for high-performance and vectorized computations on multidimensional arrays:

  `http://www.numpy.org`

- SciPy, for advanced numerical algorithms:

  `http://www.scipy.org`

- Matplotlib, for plotting and interactive visualization:

  `http://matplotlib.org`

- Matplotlib-basemap, a mapping toolbox for Matplotlib:

  `http://matplotlib.org/basemap/`

- NetworkX, for handling graphs:

  `http://networkx.lanl.gov`

- Pandas, for dealing with any kind of tabular data:

  `http://pandas.pydata.org`

- Python Imaging Library (PIL), for image-processing algorithms:

  `http://www.pythonware.com/products/pil`

- PySide, a wrapper around Qt for graphical user interfaces (GUIs):

  `http://qt-project.org/wiki/PySide`

- PyQt, similar to PySide but with a different license:

  `http://www.riverbankcomputing.co.uk/software/pyqt/intro`

- Cython, for using C code in Python:

  `http://cython.org`

PyQt or PySide?

Qt is a cross-platform application framework widely used for software with GUI. It has a complex history; originally developed by Trolltech, it was then acquired by Nokia and now owned by Digia. Both commercial and open source licenses exist. PyQt is a Qt wrapper in Python developed by Riverbank Computing. The open source version of PyQt is GPL licensed, which prevents using it in commercial products. Therefore, Nokia decided to create its own LGPL-licensed package called PySide. It is now maintained by the Qt Project. Today, both packages coexist and have an extremely similar API so that it is possible to write Qt graphical applications in Python that support both libraries.

These websites propose to download binary installers for various systems as well as the source code for manual compilation and installation.

There is also an online repository of Python packages called the Python Package Index (PyPI) available at `http://pypi.python.org`. It contains tarballs, and sometimes Windows installers, for most existing Python packages.

Getting binary installers

You may find a binary installer for your system on the official website of the packages you are interested in. If official binary installers are not available, unofficial ones may have been created by the community. We will give some advice here about where binary installers can be found on the different operating systems.

Windows

Official Windows installers may be found on the package websites or on PyPI for some packages. Unofficial Windows installers for hundreds of Python packages (including IPython and all the packages used in this book) can be found on the personal webpage of Christoph Gohlke at `http://www.lfd.uci.edu/~gohlke/pythonlibs/`. These files are provided without warranty of any kind. However, they are generally quite stable, and this makes it extremely easy to install almost any Python package on Windows. There are versions of all packages for Python 2.x and 3.x and for 32-bit and 64-bit Python distributions.

OS X

Official OS X installers can be found on the websites of some packages, and unofficial installers can be found on the MacPorts project (http://www.macports.org) and Homebrew (http://mxcl.github.com/homebrew/).

Linux

Most Linux distributions (including Ubuntu) ship with a packaging system that may contain the Python version you need along with most Python packages we will be using here. For example, to install IPython on Ubuntu, type the following command in a shell:

```
$ sudo apt-get install ipython-notebook
```

On Fedora 18 and newer related distributions, type the following command:

```
$ sudo yum install python-ipython-notebook
```

The relevant binary package names are sometimes prefixed with `python-` (for example, `python-numpy` or `python-matplotlib`). Also, PyQt4's package name is `python-qt4`, PyOpenGL's package name is `python-opengl`, PIL's package name is `python-imaging`, and so on.

Table of binary packages

We have shown here a table with the availability (at the time of writing) of binary installers for the packages we will be using in this book in the different Python distributions and operating systems. All these installers are available for Python 2.7. In the following table, "(W)" means Windows and "CG:" means Christoph Gohlke's webpage:

Package	EPD 7.3	Anaconda 1.2.1	Python (x,y) 2.7.3	Active Python 2.7.2	Windows installer	Ubuntu installer	OSX installer (MacPorts)
NetworkX	1.6	1.7	1.7	1.6	CG: 1.7	1.7	1.7
Pandas	0.9.1	0.9.0	0.9.1	0.7.3	CG: 0.10.0, PyPI: 0.10.0	0.8.0	0.10.0
NumPy	1.6.1	1.6.2 (W)	1.6.2	1.6.2	CG: 1.6.2, PyPI: 1.6.2 (32 bits)	1.6.2	1.6.2
SciPy	0.10.1	0.11.0	0.11.0	0.10.1	CG: 0.11.0	0.10.1	0.11.0
PIL	1.1.7	1.1.7	1.1.7	1.1.7	CG: 1.1.7	1.1.7	N/A

Package	EPD 7.3	Anaconda 1.2.1	Python (x,y) 2.7.3	Active Python 2.7.2	Windows installer	Ubuntu installer	OSX installer (MacPorts)
Matplotlib	1.1.0	1.2.0	1.1.1	1.1.0	CG: 1.2.0	1.1.1	1.2.0
Basemap	1.0.2	N/A	1.0.2 (optional)	1.0 beta	1.0.5	1.0.5	1.0.5
PyOpenGL	3.0.1	N/A	3.0.2	3.0.2	CG: 3.0.2, PyPI: 3.0.2	3.0.1	3.0.2
PySide	1.1.1	1.1.2	N/A (PyQt 4.9.5)	N/A (PyQt 4.8.3)	CG: 1.1.2	1.1.1	1.1.2
Cython	0.16	0.17.1	0.17.2	0.16	CG: 0.17.3	0.16	0.17.3
Numba	N/A	0.3.2	N/A	N/A	CG: 0.3.2	N/A	N/A

Using the Python packaging system

When binary packages are not available, the universal way of installing a Python package is to install it directly from its source code. The Python packaging system is meant to simplify this step so as to handle dependency management, uninstallation, and package discovery. However, the packaging system has been chaotic for years.

Distutils, the native Python packaging system, has long been criticized for being inefficient and bringing too many problems. Its successor Distutils2 is not finished at the time of writing. Setuptools is an alternative system and offers the `easy_install` command-line tool that allows searching (on PyPI) and installing new Python packages with a single command line. Installing a new package is as simple as typing in a shell:

```
$ easy_install ipython
```

Setuptools has also been criticized and is now being replaced by Distribute. The `easy_install` tool is also being replaced by pip, a more powerful tool for searching, installing, and uninstalling Python packages.

For now, we recommend that you use Distribute and pip. Both can be installed either from the source tarballs or with easy_install (which requires that you install Setuptools beforehand). More details about how to install these tools can be found on The Hitchhiker's Guide to Packaging (`http://guide.python-distribute.org/`). To install a new package with pip, type the following command in a shell:

```
$ pip install ipython
```

Optional dependencies for IPython

IPython has several dependencies:

- **pyreadline**: This dependency provides line-editing features
- **pyzmq**: This dependency is needed for IPython's parallel computing features, such as Qt console and Notebook
- **pygments**: This dependency highlights syntax in the Qt console
- **tornado**: This dependency is required by the web-based Notebook

They are all automatically installed when you install IPython from a binary package, but that is not the case when you install IPython from the source code. On Windows, pyreadline must be installed using either a binary installer available on PyPI or on Christoph Gohlke's webpage, or with easy_install or pip.

On OS X, you should also install readline with easy_install or pip.

The other dependencies can automatically be installed with the following command:

```
$ easy_install ipython[zmq,qtconsole,notebook]
```

Installing the development versions

The most experienced users may want to use the very latest development versions of some libraries. Details can be found on the websites of the respective libraries. For example, to install the development version of IPython, we can type the following command (the version control system Git needs to be installed):

```
$ git clone https://github.com/ipython/ipython.git
$ cd ipython
$ python setup.py install
```

To be able to update IPython easily as it changes on the development branch (by using git pull), we can just replace the last line with the following command (the Distribute library needs to be installed):

```
$ python setupegg.py develop
```

Getting help for IPython

The official IPython documentation webpage at http://ipython.org/documentation.html is the place to go to get some help. It contains links to the online manual and to unofficial tutorials and articles created by the community. The StackOverflow website at http://stackoverflow.com/questions/tagged/ipython is also a great place to request help for IPython. Finally, anyone can subscribe to the IPython users' mailing list http://mail.scipy.org/mailman/listinfo/ipython-user.

Ten IPython essentials

In this section, we will take a quick tour of IPython by introducing 10 essential features of this powerful tool. Although brief, this hands-on visit will cover a wide range of IPython functionality that will be explored in more detail in the next chapters.

Running the IPython console

If IPython has been installed correctly, you should be able to run it from a system shell with the ipython command. You can use this prompt like a regular Python interpreter as shown in the following screenshot:

```
PS C:\> ipython
Python 2.7.2 (default, Jun 24 2011, 12:21:10) [MSC v.1500 32 bit (Intel)]
Type "copyright", "credits" or "license" for more information.

IPython 0.14.dev -- An enhanced Interactive Python.
?         -> Introduction and overview of IPython's features.
%quickref -> Quick reference.
help      -> Python's own help system.
object?   -> Details about 'object', use 'object??' for extra details.
Qt: Untested Windows version 6.2 detected!

In [1]: print("Hello World!")
Hello World!

In [2]:
```

The IPython console

Command-line shell on Windows

If you are on Windows and using the old cmd.exe shell, you should be aware that this tool is extremely limited. You could instead use a more powerful interpreter, such as Microsoft PowerShell, which is integrated by default in Windows 7 and 8. The simple fact that most common filesystem-related commands (namely, pwd, cd, ls, cp, ps, and so on) have the same name as in Unix should be a sufficient reason to switch.

Of course, IPython offers much more than that. For example, IPython ships with tens of little commands that considerably improve productivity. We will see a lot of them in this book, starting with this section.

Some of these commands help you get information about any Python function or object. For instance, have you ever had a doubt about how to use the super function to access parent methods in a derived class? Just type super? (a shortcut for the command %pinfo super) and you will find all the information regarding the super function. Appending ? or ?? to any command or variable gives you all the information you need about it, as shown here:

```
In [1]: super?
Typical use to call a cooperative superclass method:
class C(B):
    def meth(self, arg):
        super(C, self).meth(arg)
```

Using IPython as a system shell

You can use the IPython command-line interface as an extended system shell. You can navigate throughout your filesystem and execute any system command. For instance, the standard Unix commands pwd, ls, and cd are available in IPython and work on Windows too, as shown in the following example:

```
In [1]: pwd
Out[1]: u'C:\\'
In [2]: cd windows
C:\windows
```

These commands are particular magic commands that are central in the IPython shell. There are dozens of magic commands and we will use a lot of them throughout this book. You can get a list of all magic commands with the %lsmagic command.

Using the IPython magic commands

Magic commands actually come with a % prefix, but the automagic system, enabled by default, allows you to conveniently omit this prefix. Using the prefix is always possible, particularly when the unprefixed command is shadowed by a Python variable with the same name. The %automagic command toggles the automagic system. In this book, we will generally use the % prefix to refer to magic commands, but keep in mind that you can omit it most of the time, if you prefer.

Using the history

Like the standard Python console, IPython offers a command history. However, unlike in Python's console, the IPython history spans your previous interactive sessions. In addition to this, several key strokes and commands allow you to reduce repetitive typing.

In an IPython console prompt, use the up and down arrow keys to go through your whole input history. If you start typing before pressing the arrow keys, only the commands that match what you have typed so far will be shown.

In any interactive session, your input and output history is kept in the In and Out variables and is indexed by a prompt number. The _, __, ___ and _i, _ii, _iii variables contain the last three output and input objects, respectively. The _n and _in variables return the *n*th output and input history. For instance, let's type the following command:

```
In [4]: a = 12
In [5]: a ** 2
Out[5]: 144
In [6]: print("The result is {0:d}.".format(_))
The result is 144.
```

In this example, we display the output, that is, 144 of prompt 5 on line 6.

Tab completion

Tab completion is incredibly useful and you will find yourself using it all the time. Whenever you start typing any command, variable name, or function, press the *Tab* key to let IPython either automatically complete what you are typing if there is no ambiguity, or show you the list of possible commands or names that match what you have typed so far. It also works for directories and file paths, just like in the system shell.

It is also particularly useful for dynamic object introspection. Type any Python object name followed by a point and then press the *Tab* key; IPython will show you the list of existing attributes and methods, as shown in the following example:

```
In [1]: import os
In [2]: os.path.split<TAB>
os.path.split os.path.splitdrive os.path.splitext os.path.splitunc
```

In the second line, as shown in the previous code, we press the *Tab* key after having typed os.path.split. IPython then displays all the possible commands.

Tab Completion and Private Variables

Tab completion shows you all the attributes and methods of an object, except those that begin with an underscore (_). The reason is that it is a standard convention in Python programming to prefix private variables with an underscore. To force IPython to show all private attributes and methods, type myobject._ before pressing the *Tab* key. Nothing is really private or hidden in Python. It is part of a general Python philosophy, as expressed by the famous saying, "We are all consenting adults here."

Executing a script with the %run command

Although essential, the interactive console becomes limited when running sequences of multiple commands. Writing multiple commands in a Python script with the .py file extension (by convention) is quite common. A Python script can be executed from within the IPython console with the %run magic command followed by the script filename. The script is executed in a fresh, new Python namespace unless the -i option has been used, in which case the current interactive Python namespace is used for the execution. In all cases, all variables defined in the script become available in the console at the end of script execution.

Let's write the following Python script in a file called script.py:

```
print("Running script.")
x = 12
print("'x' is now equal to {0:d}.".format(x))
```

Now, assuming we are in the directory where this file is located, we can execute it in IPython by entering the following command:

```
In [1]: %run script.py
Running script.
'x' is now equal to 12.
In [2]: x
Out[2]: 12
```

When running the script, the standard output of the console displays any print statement. At the end of execution, the x variable defined in the script is then included in the interactive namespace, which is quite convenient.

Quick benchmarking with the %timeit command

You can do quick benchmarks in an interactive session with the %timeit magic command. It lets you estimate how much time the execution of a single command takes. The same command is executed multiple times within a loop, and this loop itself is repeated several times by default. The individual execution time of the command is then automatically estimated with an average. The -n option controls the number of executions in a loop, whereas the -r option controls the number of executed loops. For example, let's type the following command:

```
In[1]: %timeit [x*x for x in range(100000)]
10 loops, best of 3: 26.1 ms per loop
```

Here, it took about 26 milliseconds to compute the squares of all integers up to 100000.

Quick debugging with the %debug command

IPython ships with a powerful command-line debugger. Whenever an exception is raised in the console, use the %debug magic command to launch the debugger at the exception point. You then have access to all the local variables and to the full stack traceback in postmortem mode. Navigate up and down through the stack with the u and d commands and exit the debugger with the q command. See the list of all the available commands in the debugger by entering the ? command.

You can use the %pdb magic command to activate the automatic execution of the IPython debugger as soon as an exception is raised.

Interactive computing with Pylab

The `%pylab` magic command enables the scientific computing capabilities of the NumPy and matplotlib packages, namely efficient operations on vectors and matrices and plotting and interactive visualization features. It becomes possible to perform interactive computations in the console and plot graphs dynamically. For example, let's enter the following command:

```
In [1]: %pylab
Welcome to pylab, a matplotlib-based Python environment [backend: TkAgg].
For more information, type 'help(pylab)'.
In [2]: x = linspace(-10., 10., 1000)
In [3]: plot(x, sin(x))
```

In this example, we first define a vector of `1000` values linearly spaced between `-10` and `10`. Then we plot the graph `(x, sin(x))`. A window with a plot appears as shown in the following screenshot, and the console is not blocked while this window is opened. This allows us to interactively modify the plot while it is open.

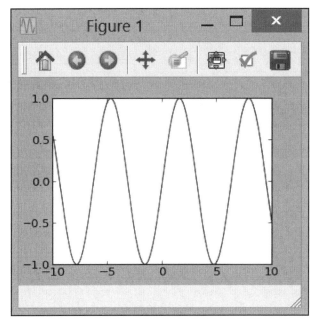

A Matplotlib figure

Using the IPython Notebook

The Notebook brings the functionality of IPython into the browser for multiline text-editing features, interactive session reproducibility, and so on. It is a modern and powerful way of using Python in an interactive and reproducible way.

To use the Notebook, call the `ipython notebook` command in a shell (make sure you have installed the required dependencies described in the Installation section). This will launch a local web server on the default port 8888. Go to `http://127.0.0.1:8888/` in a browser and create a new Notebook.

You can write one or several lines of code in the input cells. Here are some of the most useful keyboard shortcuts:

- Press the *Enter* key to create a new line in the cell and not execute the cell
- Press *Shift* + *Enter* to execute the cell and go to the next cell
- Press *Alt* + *Enter* to execute the cell and append a new empty cell right after it
- Press *Ctrl* + *Enter* for quick instant experiments when you do not want to save the output
- Press *Ctrl* + *M* and then the *H* key to display the list of all the keyboard shortcuts

We will explore the features of the Notebook more thoroughly in the next chapter.

Customizing IPython

You can save your user preferences in a Python file; this file is called an IPython profile. To create a default profile, type `ipython profile create` in a shell. This will create a folder named `profile_default` in the `~/.ipython` or `~/.config/ipython` directory. The file `ipython_config.py` in this folder contains preferences about IPython. You can create different profiles with different names using `ipython profile create profilename`, and then launch IPython with `ipython --profile=profilename` to use that profile.

The ~ directory is your home directory, for example, something like `/home/yourname` on Unix, or `C:\Users\yourname` or `C:\Documents and Settings\yourname` on Windows.

Summary

In this chapter, we have detailed the various ways with which you can install IPython and the recommended external Python packages. The most straightforward way is to install a standalone Python distribution with all packages built in, such as Enthought Python Distribution or Canopy, Anaconda, Python(x,y), or ActivePython, among others. The other solution is to install the different packages manually, either with binary installers available for most recent platforms, or by using the Python packaging system, which should be straightforward in most cases.

We have also gone through 10 of the most interesting features offered by IPython. They essentially concern the Python and shell interactive features, including the integrated debugger and profiler, and the interactive computing and visualization features brought by the NumPy and Matplotlib packages. In the following chapter, we will detail the interactive shell and Python console as well as the Notebook.

2
Interactive Work with IPython

In this chapter, we will detail the various improvements that IPython brings to the standard Python console. In particular, we will perform the following tasks:

- Access the system shell from IPython for powerful interactions between the shell and Python
- Use dynamic introspection to explore Python objects or even a new Python package without even the need to look at the documentation
- Easily debug and benchmark your code from IPython
- Learn how to use the IPython notebook to improve considerably the way you interact with Python

The extended shell

IPython is not only an extended Python console, but it also provides several ways to interact with the operating system during a Python interactive session without quitting the console. The shell features of IPython are not meant to replace the Unix shell, and IPython offers far less features. Yet, it is still quite convenient to be able to navigate through the filesystem during a Python session and to occasionally call system commands from IPython. Moreover, IPython provides useful magic commands that considerably improve productivity and reduce repetitive typing during an interactive session.

Navigating through the filesystem

Here, we will show how we can download and extract compressed files from the Internet, navigate in a filesystem hierarchy, and open text files from IPython. To do this, we will use an example with real data about the social networks of hundreds of anonymous people on Facebook (who volunteered to share their data anonymously to computer scientists for research purposes). This BSD-licensed data are provided freely by the SNAP project from Stanford University (http://snap.stanford.edu/data/).

Downloading the example code

You can download the example code files for all Packt books that you have purchased from your account at http://www.packtpub.com. If you purchased this book elsewhere, you can visit http://www.packtpub.com/support and register to have the files e-mailed directly to you. In addition, all examples can be downloaded from the author's website: http://ipython.rossant.net.

First, we need to download the ZIP file containing the data from the author's webpage. We use the native Python module urllib2 to download the file, and the zipfile module to extract it. Let's enter the following commands:

```
In [1]: import urllib2, zipfile
In [2]: url = 'http://ipython.rossant.net/'
In [3]: filename = 'facebook.zip'
In [4]: downloaded = urllib2.urlopen(url + filename)
```

Here, we downloaded the file http://ipython.rossant.net/facebook.zip in the memory, and we are going to save it on the hard drive.

Now, we create a new folder named data in the current directory, and we enter it. The dollar ($) sign allows us to use a Python variable within a system or magic command. Let's enter the following commands:

```
In [5]: folder = 'data'
In [6]: mkdir $folder
In [7]: cd $folder
```

Here, `mkdir` is a particular IPython *alias* redirecting a magic command to a shell command. The list of aliases can be obtained with the magic `%alias` command. In this folder, we are going to save the file we have just downloaded (in line eight, we locally save the ZIP file in `facebook.zip` in the current directory `data`), and extract it in the current folder (as shown in line nine, with the `extractall` method of `zip` and a `ZipFile` object). Let's enter the following commands:

```
In [8]: with open(filename, 'wb') as f:
            f.write(downloaded.read())
In [9]: with zipfile.ZipFile(filename) as zip:
            zip.extractall('.')
```

Let's explore what we have just downloaded using the following commands:

```
In [10]: ls
facebook   facebook.zip
In [11]: cd facebook
In [12]: ls
0.circles   0.edges   [...]
```

In this example, each number identifies a Facebook user (called the `ego` user). The `.edges` file contains its *social graph*, that is, the graph where each node is a friend, and two friends of the `ego` user are connected if they are friends of each other. This graph is stored as an `edges` list, a text file where each line contains two connected nodes' identifiers separated by a space. The `.circles` file contains manually-created friends' lists, that is, the groups of friends that share common attributes from the `ego` user's viewpoint.

Finally, we save the current `facebook` directory as a bookmark using the following command so we can easily enter into this directory later:

```
In [13]: %bookmark fbdata
```

Now, in any future session with the same IPython profile, we can type `cd fbdata` to enter into this directory, whichever directory we call this command from. The `-l` and `-d` options allow to respectively list all defined bookmarks, and delete a specified bookmark. Typing `%bookmark?` displays the list of all options. This magic command can be really helpful when navigating back and forth between several folders.

Another convenient navigation-related function in IPython is *tab* completion. IPython can automatically complete the file or folder name we are typing if we press the *Tab* key. If several options are possible, IPython will show us the list of all possible options. It also works with filenames, for instance, in the open built-in function, as shown in the following example:

```
In [1]: pwd
/home/me/data/
In [2]: cd fa<TAB>
/home/me/data/facebook/
In [2]: cd facebook
In [3]: with open('0<TAB>
0.circles    0.edges
In [3]: with open('0.edges', 'r') as f:
            print(f.readline())
236 186
```

Accessing the system shell from IPython

We can also launch commands using the system shell directly from IPython, and retrieve the result as a list of strings in a Python variable. To do this, we need to prefix shell commands with !. For example, assuming that we are using a Unix system, we can type the following commands:

```
In [1]: cd fbdata
/home/me/data/facebook
In [2]: files = !ls -1 -S | grep edges
```

The Unix command ls -1 -S lists all files in the current directory, sorted by decreasing size, and with one file per line. The pipe | grep edges filters only those files that contain edges (these are the files with social graphs of different networks). Then, the Python variable files contains the list of all filenames, as shown in the following example:

```
In [3]: files
Out[3]: ['1912.edges',
  '107.edges',
  [...]
  '3980.edges']
```

We can also use Python variables in the system command, using either the $ syntax for single variables, or { } for any Python expression, as follows:

```
In [4]: !head -n5 {files[0]}
2290 2363
2346 2025
2140 2428
2201 2506
2425 2557
```

The head -n5 {files[0]} command displays the first five lines of the first file in the files list, that is, the first five lines of the largest .edges file in the dataset.

If we find ourselves using the same command over and over, we can create an **alias** to save some repetitive typing, using the magic %alias command. For instance, in the following example we create an alias called largest that is used to display on a single column (-1) all files with their sizes (-hs), filtered with a specified string (grep) and ordered by their decreasing size (-S):

```
In [5]: %alias largest ls -1sSh | grep %s
in [6]: largest circles
6.0K 1912.circles
4.0K 1684.circles
[...]
```

In line five, note the %s positional placeholder for the largest alias, which will be replaced by any argument given to the alias (as shown in line six).

Note that, by default, this alias will not be saved for future use in the next interactive sessions (after closing IPython). We need to save it explicitly with the %store magic command as follows:

```
In [7]: %store largest
Alias stored: largest (ls -1sSh | grep %s)
```

In addition, to recover the stored aliases and variables in a later session, we will need to type %store -r.

The extended Python console

We will now explore the Python-related capabilities of the **IPython** console.

Exploring the history

IPython keeps track of all our input history across all sessions. Since this history can become quite large after months or years of working with IPython, there are convenient ways of navigating through it.

First, we can press the up and down keys at any time in the IPython prompt to navigate linearly through our recent history. If we type something before pressing the up and down keys, we only navigate through the input commands that match what we have typed so far. Pressing *Ctrl + R* opens a prompt that allows us to search for a line that contains whatever we type in this prompt.

The %history magic command (and %hist, which is an alias) accepts multiple convenient options to display the part of the input history we are interested in. By default, %history displays all our input history in the current session. We can specify a specific line range with a simple syntax, for example, hist 4-6 8 for lines four to six and line eight. We can also choose to display our history from the previous sessions with the syntax hist 243/4-8 for lines four to eight in session 243. Finally, we can number the sessions relative to the current session using the syntax %hist ~1/7, which shows line seven of the previous session.

Other useful options for %history include -o, which displays the output in addition to the input; -n, which displays the line numbers; -f, which saves the history to a file; and -p, which displays the classic >>> prompt. For example, this can prove to be useful for automatically creating a doctest file from the history. Also, the -g option allows to filter the history with a specified string (like grep). Consider the following example:

```
In [1]: 2 + 3
Out[1]: 5
In [2]: _ * 2
Out[2]: 10
In [3]: %hist -nop 1-2
  1: >>> 2 + 3
5
  2: >>> _ * 2
10
```

In this example, we display the history of the first two lines with the line number, the output, and the default Python prompt.

Finally, a related command is %store, which is used to save the content of any Python variable for later use in any future interactive session. The %store name command saves the variable name, and %store -d name deletes it. To recover the stored variables, we need to use %store -r.

Import/export of Python code

In the following section, we will first see how to import code from a Python script in the interactive console, and then how to export code from the history into an external file.

Importing code in IPython

A first possibility to import code in IPython is to copy and paste code from a file to IPython. When using the **IPython** console, the `%paste` magic command can be used to import and execute the code contained in the clipboard. IPython automatically dedents the code and removes the > and + characters at the beginning of the lines, allowing to paste the `diff` and `doctest` files directly from e-mails.

In addition, the `%run` magic command executes a Python script in the console, by default, in an empty namespace. It means that any variable defined in the interactive namespace is not available within the executed script. However, at the end of the execution, the control returns to IPython's prompt, and the variables defined in the script are then imported in the interactive namespace. This is very convenient for exploring the state of all variables at the end of the script's execution. This behavior can be changed with the `-i` option, which uses the interactive namespace for the execution. The variables defined in the interactive namespace before the script's execution are then available in the script.

For example, let's write a script `/home/me/data/egos.py` that lists all ego identifiers in Facebook's `data` folder. Since each filename is of the form `<egoid>.<extension>`, we list all the files, remove the extensions, and take the sorted list of all unique identifiers. The script should contain the following code:

```
import sys
import os
# we retrieve the folder as the first positional argument
# to the command-line call
if len(sys.argv) > 1:
    folder = sys.argv[1]
# we list all files in the specified folder
files = os.listdir(folder)
# ids contains the sorted list of all unique idenfitiers
ids = sorted(set(map(lambda file: int(file.split('.')[0]), files)))
```

Here is an explanation of what the last line does. The `lambda` function takes a filename as an argument following the template `<egoid>.<extension>`, and returns the `egoid` ID as an integer. It uses the `split` method of any string, which splits a string with a given character and returns a list of substrings, which are separated by this character. Here, the first element of the list is the `<egoid>` part. The `map` built-in Python function applies this `lambda` function to all filenames. The `set` function converts this list to a `set` object, thereby removing all duplicates and keeping only a list of unique identifiers (since any identifier appears twice with two different extensions). Finally, the `sorted` function converts the `set` object to a list, and sorts it in an increasing order.

Assuming the current directory in IPython is `/home/me/data`, following is the command to execute this script:

```
In [1]: %run egos.py facebook
In [2]: ids
Out[2]: [0, 107, ..., 3980]
```

In the `egos.py` script, the folder name `facebook` is retrieved from the command-line arguments, like in a standard command-line Python script, with `sys.argv[1]`. After the script has been executed, the `ids` variable defined in the script is available in the interactive namespace, and contains the list of unique `ego` identifiers.

Now, following is what happens if we do not provide the folder name as an argument to the script:

```
In [3]: folder = 'facebook'
In [4]: %run egos.py
NameError: name 'folder' is not defined
In [5]: %run -i egos.py
In [6]: ids
Out[6]: [0, 107, ..., 3980]
```

An exception is raised in line four since `folder` is not defined. If we want the script to use the `folder` variable defined in the interactive namespace, we need to use the `-i` option.

Interactive workflow in exploratory research

A standard workflow in exploratory research or in data analysis is to implement algorithms in one or several Python modules and write a script that executes the full process. This script can then be executed with %run and allows further interactive exploration of the script variables. This iterative process involves switching between a text editor and the **IPython** console. A more modern and practical approach is to use the IPython notebook, as we will see in the section *Using the IPython notebook*.

Exporting code to a file

While the %run magic command allows to import code from a file to the interactive console, the %edit command does the opposite. By default, %edit opens the system's text editor and executes the code when we close the editor. If we supply an argument to %edit, this command will try to open the text editor with the code we supplied. The argument can be as follows:

- A Python script filename
- A string variable containing Python code
- A range of line numbers, with the same syntax of %history, which was used previously
- Any Python object, in which case IPython will try to open the editor with the file where this object has been defined

A more modern and powerful way of using a multiline text editor with IPython is to use the notebook, as we will see in the *Using the IPython notebook* section.

Dynamic introspection

IPython offers several features for dynamically inspecting Python objects in the namespace.

Tab completion

At any time, we can type TAB in the console to let IPython either complete or propose a list of possible names or commands that match what we have typed so far. This allows, in particular, to dynamically inspect all attributes and methods of any Python object.

Tab completion also works for global variables in the interactive namespace, modules, and file paths in the current directory. By default, variables that begin with _ (underscore) are not shown, because it is a Python convention to prefix private variables with an underscore. However, typing _ before pressing *Tab* forces IPython to display all private variables.

An example of tab completion NetworkX

Here, we will use tab completion to find out how we can load and manipulate a graph with the *NetworkX* package. This package is commonly used when working with graphs. Let's execute the following command to import the package:

```
In [1]: import networkx as nx
```

To find the available options for opening a graph, we can look for the possible methods prefixed with read, as follows:

```
In [2]: nx.read<TAB>
nx.read_adjlist   nx.read_dot   nx.read_edgelist   [...]
```

Since the .edges files contain a list of edges, we try the following command (assuming we are in the fbdata folder):

```
In [3]: g = nx.read_edgelist('0.edges')
```

Now that the graph g appears to be loaded, we can explore the methods offered by this new object, as follows:

```
In [4]: g.<TAB>
g.add_cycle   [...]   g.edges   [...]   g.nodes
In [5]: len(g.nodes()), len(g.edges())
Out[5]: (333, 2519)
```

The 0 ego user then appears to have 333 friends, and there are 2519 connections between these friends.

Let's explore the structure of this graph a bit more. How well connected are any two users in this graph? The theory of small-world graphs predicts that any two persons are about six links away in a social graph. Here, we can compute the *radius* and *diameter* of the graph, that is, the minimum and maximum path length between any two nodes. Tab completion shows that there is a radius method in the NetworkX package. So, we try the following command:

```
In [6]: nx.radius(g)
[...]
NetworkXError: Graph not connected: infinite path length
```

Our graph appears to be disconnected since the radius and diameter are not well defined. To work around this problem, we can take a connected component of the graph, as follows:

```
In [7]: nx.connected<TAB>
nx.connected  nx.connected_component_subgraphs  [...]
```

The second proposition looks like a good choice (hence, the importance of choosing good names when creating a package!), as shown in the following commands:

```
In [8]: sg = nx.connected_component_subgraphs(g)
In [9]: [len(s) for s in sg]
Out[9]: [324, 3, 2, 2, 2]
In [10]: sg = sg[0]
In [11]: nx.radius(sg), nx.diameter(sg)
Out[11]: (6, 11)
```

There are five connected components; we take the largest one and compute its radius and diameter. Hence, any two friends are connected through less than 11 levels, and there is one friend that is less than six links away from any other friend.

Tab completion with custom classes

If we define our own classes, we can customize the way their instances work with IPython tab completion. All we have to do is override the __dir__ method to return the list of attributes as shown in the following commands:

```
In [12]: class MyClass(object):
            def __dir__(self):
                return ['attr1', 'attr2']
In [13]: obj = MyClass()
In [14]: obj.<TAB>
obj.attr1  obj.attr2
```

This feature can be useful in some scenarios where the list of interesting attributes of an instance is defined dynamically.

Source code introspection

IPython can also display information about the internals of a variable, in particular about the source code when it is defined in a file. First, typing ? before or after a variable name prints useful information about it. Typing ?? gives more detailed information, in particular, the source code of the object, if it is a function defined in a file.

In addition, several magic commands display specific information about a variable, such as the source code of the function (%psource) or of the file (%pfile) where it is defined, the docstring (%pdoc), or the definition header (%pdef).

The %pfile magic command also accepts a Python filename, in which case, it prints the file's contents with syntax highlighting. With this function, IPython can then act as a code viewer with syntax highlighting.

Using the interactive debugger

For most of us, debugging is an important part of the programming job. IPython makes it extremely convenient to debug a script or an entire application. It provides interactive access to an enhanced version of the Python debugger.

First, when we encounter an exception, we can use the %debug magic command to launch the IPython debugger at the exact point where the exception was raised. If we activate the %pdb magic command, the debugger will be automatically launched upon the very next exception. We can also start IPython with ipython --pdb for the same behavior. Finally, we can run a whole script under the control of the debugger with the %run -d command. This command executes the specified script with a break point at the first line so that we can precisely control the execution flow of the script. We can also specify explicitly where to put the first breakpoint; typing %run -d -b29 script.py pauses the program execution on line 29 of script.py. We first need to type c to start the script execution.

When the debugger launches, the prompt becomes ipdb>. The program execution is then paused at a given point in the code. We can use the w command to display the line and the location in the stack traceback where the debugger has paused. At this point, we have access to all local variables and we can control precisely how we want to resume the execution. Within the debugger, several commands are available to navigate into the traceback:

- u/d for going *up/down* into the call stack
- s to *step* into the next statement
- n to continue execution until the *next line* in the current function
- r to continue execution until the current function *returns*
- c to *continue* execution until the next breakpoint or exception

Other useful commands include:

- p to evaluate and *print* any expression
- a to obtain the *arguments* of the current functions
- The ! prefix to execute any Python command within the debugger

The entire list of commands can be found in the documentation of the pdb module in Python.

Interactive benchmarking and profiling

Donald Knuth said:

> *"Premature optimization is the root of all evil."*

This means that optimization should only occur in case of absolute necessity, and if the code has been thoroughly profiled so that you know exactly what portion of the code needs to be optimized. IPython makes this benchmarking and profiling process easy.

Controlling the execution time of a command

First, the %timeit magic function uses the Python's timeit module to estimate the execution time of any Python statement. If we have defined a function fun(x), %timeit fun(x) executes this command multiple times and returns an average of the execution time. The number of calls is determined automatically; there are r loops of n executions each. These numbers can be specified with the -r and -n options to %timeit. Also, we can easily estimate the execution time of a script with the %run -t command.

In the following example, we compute the *center* of sg, that is, the set of nodes with eccentricity equal to the radius (that is, the friends in the ego circle who are the most well connected to all other friends), and estimate the time it takes:

```
In [19]: %timeit nx.center(sg)
1 loops, best of 3: 377 ms per loop
In [20]: nx.center(sg)
Out[20]: [u'51', u'190', u'83', u'307', u'175', u'237', u'277', u'124']
```

We can see in the previous example that it took 377 milliseconds for Python and NetworkX to compute the center of sg. The center function has been called three times (best of 3 in the output 19), and the smallest time of execution has been automatically selected (since the very first execution can take longer, due to some Python imports, for instance).

Profiling a script

To obtain much more detailed information about the execution time of a program, we can execute it under the control of a *profiler*, like the one provided natively by the profile Python module. Profiling is a complex topic, and we are just going to show a basic usage example here. More details about the profile module can be found in the official Python documentation.

To run a script under the control of the profiler, we can execute it from IPython with %run -p or with the equivalent %prun magic command.

Here, we will write a small Python script that computes the center of the graph without using the built-in NetworkX center function. Let's create a script called center.py with the following code:

```
import networkx as nx
g = nx.read_edgelist('0.edges')
sg = nx.connected_component_subgraphs(g)[0]
center = [node for node in sg.nodes() if nx.eccentricity(sg, node) ==
nx.radius(sg)]
print(center)
```

Now, let's run it and estimate the time it takes using the following commands:

```
In [21]: %run -t center.py
[u'51', u'190', u'83', u'307', u'175', u'237', u'277', u'124']
IPython CPU timings (estimated):
  User   :      128.36 s.
```

This script took more than two minutes to execute; this looks particularly bad! We can run the profiler with the command %run -p center.py to find out what is taking so long.

The profiler outputs details about calls of every Python function used directly or indirectly in this script. For example, the cumtime column prints the cumulative time spent within every function. It appears, from the previous example, that eccentricity and radius are the major bottlenecks, because they are called 648 and 324 times, respectively! Looking more closely at the code shows that we are indeed doing something stupid; that is, we are calling these two functions repetitively within the loop. We can considerably improve the performance of this script by *caching* the output of these functions. Let's modify the script in center2.py:

```
import networkx as nx
g = nx.read_edgelist('data/facebook/0.edges')
sg = nx.connected_component_subgraphs(g)[0]
# we compute the eccentricity once, for all nodes
```

```
ecc = nx.eccentricity(sg)
# we compute the radius once
r = nx.radius(sg)
center = [node for node in sg.nodes() if ecc[node] == r]
print(center)
```

Here, we compute the eccentricity of all nodes with a single call to `eccentricity` before the loop, and we compute the radius of the graph only once. Let's check the performance of this improved script by executing the following commands:

```
In [23]: %run -t center2.py
[u'51', u'190', u'83', u'307', u'175', u'237', u'277', u'124']
IPython CPU timings (estimated):
  User   :       0.88 s.
```

With this modification, our computation takes less than a second instead of two minutes! Of course, even if this example was a particularly trivial one, this kind of mistake can be made by any programmer at some point in a long program. Then, it may not be so obvious to find this bottleneck just by reading the code. The best way to find such hotspots is to use a profiler, and IPython makes this task particularly easy.

Using a line-by-line profiler

For even more fine-grained profiling, we can use a line-by-line profiler. This tool analyzes the time taken by every single line in a set of functions chosen by the programmer. In Python, the `line_profiler` package does exactly this. The functions to profile are indicated with a `@profile` decorator. Its usage is less straightforward than the IPython profiler, and we invite the interested reader to check out the package's website at http://packages.python.org/line_profiler/. We will also mention it in *Chapter 6, Customizing IPython*.

Using the IPython notebook

The IPython notebook is increasingly used in the Python community, in particular for scientific research and education. It brings both a powerful HTML user interface to IPython and a way of saving a whole interactive session in a notebook file in a JSON format. The latter functionality brings reproducibility to interactive computing, a crucial feature notably in scientific research. Notebooks run in the browser and can contain, not only Python code, but also text in a markup language, such as Markdown, as well as images, videos, or rich content media. Notebooks can be converted into other formats, such as Python scripts, HTML, or PDF. Courses, blog posts, and books are being written with the notebook.

IPython Qt console

There is another rich IPython frontend similar to the notebook that is based on Qt instead of HTML. You can find more information about it at `http://ipython.org/ipython-doc/stable/interactive/qtconsole.html`.

Installation

The IPython notebook server requires several dependencies. If you use either a full distribution, or if you have installed IPython from a binary package, you should have nothing more to do. If you have installed IPython manually, you will need PyZMQ and Tornado. PyZMQ is a Python wrapper to the ZMQ socket library, whereas Tornado is a Python library implementing the HTTP server that the notebook uses. You can install these packages either with `easy_install`, `pip`, or from the source.

The notebook dashboard

To check that everything is correctly installed, type `ipython notebook` in a shell. This will launch a local web server on the 8888 port (by default). Go to `http://127.0.0.1:8888/` in a browser and check if you can see the following page:

The notebook dashboard

Browser compatibility with the notebook

The IPython notebook is compatible with browsers such as Chrome, Safari, Firefox 6 and later versions, and Internet Explorer 10 and later versions. These browsers support the **WebSocket** protocol, which is used by the notebook.

The page in the previous screenshot is the **notebook dashboard**; it lists all notebooks in the directory where we launched `ipython notebook` from. An IPython notebook file has a `.ipynb` extension; it is a text file containing structured data in JSON.

This file contains the inputs and outputs of an interaction session, as well as some metadata used by IPython internally.

 Viewing notebooks online

IPython notebooks can be viewed and shared online on the IPython Notebook Viewer available at http://nbviewer.ipython.org/.

Let's start and create a new notebook. Click on the **New Notebook** button at the top-right of the page.

Working with cells

We are now in a notebook. The user interface is clean and focuses on the essential features. At the top, the menu and the toolbar offer access to all commands. The main area below them shows, by default, an empty input cell. Python code can be typed into this input cell. An important feature of an input cell is that pressing the *Enter* key does not execute the cell, but rather inserts a new line. Writing code into a cell is then closer to what a standard text editor offers, compared to the classic **IPython** console.

Start typing the command as shown in the following screenshot, and note how tab completion is implemented:

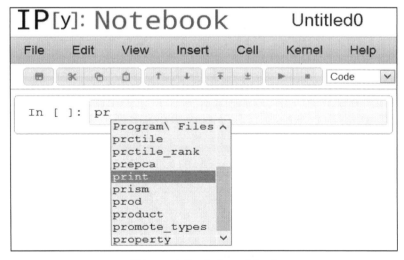

Tab completion in the notebook

An input cell can be executed in two ways. By pressing *Shift + Enter*, all the code within the cell is executed in the current IPython interactive namespace. The output then appears in an output area right below the input cell, and a new input cell is created below. By pressing *Ctrl + Enter*, no new input cell is created and only the output is shown. Typically, we will use the latter command for quick in-place experiments when we just need to evaluate some Python expression and we do not want to save the cell's output in the notebook (although we can always delete cells later).

In the end, a notebook contains a linear succession of input and output cells, representing a coherent and reproducible interactive session. Typically, a single cell contains a set of instructions, which perform some high-level action that requires several consecutive commands.

The interface offers commands to edit, delete, split, and merge cells. These commands can be accessed through the menu, the toolbar, or keyboard shortcuts. We can display the list of all keyboard shortcuts by pressing *Ctrl + M*, then *H*. Most notebook commands are executed with a sequence of keystrokes that begin with *Ctrl + M*, followed by a single key press.

Cell magics

Cell magics are special magic commands that are applied to a whole cell instead of a single line. They are prefixed with `%%` instead of `%`, and can be used either in the **IPython** console, or in the IPython notebook. The list of all cell magics can be obtained with the command `%lsmagic`. Two useful cell magics include `%%!` for executing several system shell commands from IPython, and `%%file` for creating a text file, as shown in the following example:

```
In [1]: %%file test.txt
        Hello World!
Writing test.txt
In [2]: %%!
        more test.txt
Out[2]: ['Hello World!']
```

Managing notebooks

We can save the notebook we are working on at any time by clicking on the **Save** button or by pressing *Ctrl + S* or *Ctrl + M*, then *S*. By default, the notebook filename is Untitled0, but we can rename it with the Rename command in the **File** menu.

We can create a new notebook from an existing Python script by dragging the Python file from the system explorer to the IPython dashboard. This will create a new notebook with the same name as our script, but with a .ipynb extension. A notebook can be downloaded as a Python script or as a .ipynb file.

Multimedia and rich text editing

A very useful feature of the notebook is the possibility to insert rich text in cells using a popular marker text format called **Markdown** (described at http://daringfireball.net/projects/markdown/syntax). Edition features such as bold, italic, headers, and bullet points can be inserted with a simple syntax. To do this, we need to convert a cell into a **Markdown** cell with the Cell > Markdown command.

Then, we can type our text with the Markdown syntax. If we press *Shift + Enter*, the text will be automatically formatted, and it can be edited with a double-click. The following screenshot shows both the Markdown code and the corresponding formatted text:

```
Hello World example
===================

In this example we'll learn how to:

  * **convert a cell** in [Markdown]
(http://daringfireball.net/projects/markdown/)
  * display formatted text with Markdown
```

Hello World example

In this example we'll learn how to:

- **convert a cell** in Markdown
- display formatted text with Markdown

Markdown input and output in the notebook

Graph plotting

Let's illustrate the plotting capabilities of the notebook with our social network example. We are going to draw the graph sg. First, we need to launch the notebook with the command `ipython notebook --pylab inline`. This option will be covered in more detail in *Chapter 4, Figures and Graphical Interfaces*. It allows to insert figures within the notebook, thanks to the Matplotlib library. NetworkX offers several Matplotlib-based commands to plot graphs. In the following example, we use the `draw_networkx` function to draw the graph sg, along with several parameters to improve the readability of the graph (the full list of options can be found on the NetworkX documentation website):

```
nx.draw_networkx(sg, node_size=15,
edge_color='y', with_labels=False,
alpha=.4, linewidths=0)
```

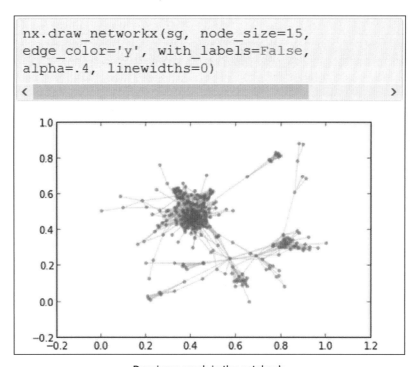

Drawing a graph in the notebook

Summary

We now have a broad overview of the features that IPython offers to simplify and extend the way we interact with IPython in our day-to-day programming job. From the powerful Python history to the essential dynamic introspection features, deciding whether to use IPython or the standard Python console for interactive programming is a no-brainer. Also, the notebook offers a modern way of using IPython for a wide variety of uses, such as simply recording an interactive session and creating a programming course, a presentation, or even a book!

Yet, what IPython offers does not stop here. It really comes into its own when using it with external packages offering numerical computing and visualization features: NumPy, SciPy, Matplotlib, and others. These packages can absolutely be used without IPython. However, using IPython fully makes sense since it then allows *interactive* numerical computing and visualization with the Python programming language. Together, these tools are becoming the platform of choice for open-source scientific computing, even competing with the widespread commercial solutions of reference. In the next chapter, we will cover the numerical computing capabilities of the platform.

3
Numerical Computing with IPython

Although IPython's powerful shell and extended console can be advantageously used by any Python programmer, this package was originally a tool designed *for scientists by scientists*. It was indeed meant to provide a convenient way of doing *interactive scientific computing* with Python.

IPython does not really provide scientific computing features *per se*, but rather offers an interactive interface to powerful external libraries, such as NumPy, SciPy, Pandas, Matplotlib, and the like. Together, these tools provide a framework for scientific computing, which can compete with widespread commercial tools in the scientific community such as Matlab or Mathematica.

NumPy provides a multidimensional array object that supports optimized vector operations. SciPy offers a wide variety of scientific algorithms (signal processing, optimization, and so on) that are based on NumPy. Pandas proposes convenient data structures for tabular data coming from real-world data sets. Matplotlib allows to plot graphical figures easily so as to visualize interactively any form of data, and to generate publication-quality figures. IPython provides the adequate interactive framework for using all these tools in a streamlined way.

In this section, we will:

- Explore the interactive computing possibilities offered by NumPy and Pandas
- Understand why multidimensional arrays are well adapted to high-performance computations
- See how arrays can be used in practical applications
- Find some references containing more advanced examples and applications

A primer to vector computing

In this section we will introduce the notion of **vectorized computations**. It is an absolutely crucial notion since it is the easiest way to achieve high performance with a high-level language such as Python.

An example of computation with Python loops

Today's science and engineering are all about numbers. Most data processing and numerical simulations are nothing else but a succession of elementary operations on large amounts of numerical data, and computers are extremely good at it. However, data has to be structured in some rational way. The generic structure of numerical data is that of *vectors* and *matrices*, and more generally *multidimensional arrays*.

Before we explain in more detail what a numerical array is, let's take a look at an example motivating the introduction of these objects. Let's suppose we have retrieved geographical data with the coordinates (latitude and longitude) of a large number of locations, and we need to find the location that is the closest to a given position of interest. For example, we may want to find the closest restaurant from the GPS position of a smartphone user.

If the positions are stored in a Python list of tuples, we can write something like the following code:

```
def closest(position, positions):
    x0, y0 = position
    dbest, ibest = None, None
    for i, (x, y) in enumerate(positions):
        # squared Euclidean distance from every position to the
position of interest
        d = (x - x0) ** 2 + (y - y0) ** 2
        if dbest is None or d < dbest:
            dbest, ibest = d, i
    return ibest
```

Here, we loop through all positions. The variable i keeps the index of the current position, whereas (x, y) contains the coordinates of this position. The position of interest is position=(x0, y0). At the first iteration, the current position is recorded as the best so far, and at the next iterations, the closest position is updated only if the current position is closer than the closest one so far. At the end of the loop, the index of the closest location is ibest, the corresponding position is positions[ibest], and the squared distance from the position of interest to the closest position is in dbest. To compute the distances, we use here the squared Euclidean distance formula, $D = (x - x0)^2 + (y - y0)^2$.

This is a standard and basic algorithm. Let's evaluate its performance on a large dataset. We first generate a list of 10 million random positions as follows:

```
In [1]: import random
```

```
In [2]: positions = [(random.random(), random.random()) for _ in
xrange(10000000)]
```

We defined a list named positions with pairs of coordinates, each number being a random number between zero and one. Now, let's set some benchmark using the following command:

```
In [3]: %timeit closest((.5, .5), positions)
```

```
1 loops, best of 3: 16.4 s per loop.
```

This algorithm took 16.4 seconds to process 10 million positions. Let's see if that is close to the theoretical maximum performance of a CPU. This code was executed on a 2 GHz single core processor. It can theoretically process four floating point operations per cycle, corresponding to eight billion operations per second. In our algorithm, each iteration involves five mathematical operations and a comparison, for a total of 50 million floating point operations (taking only the mathematical operations into account). The theoretical maximum performance should have been 6.25 ms. This means that our algorithm performed about 2,600 times worse than the theoretical maximum performance!

Of course, this is a very naive estimation, and the theoretical maximum performance is always far from being reached, but a discrepancy factor of 2,600 seems particularly bad. Can we do better? We will find out in the next section.

What an array is

In the previous example, the same computation (computing the distance to a fixed point) was performed on a lot of numbers. NumPy provides a new type that is perfectly adapted to this situation: the **multidimensional array**. So, what is an array?

An array is a block of data organized into several dimensions. A one-dimensional array is a vector, which is an ordered sequence of elements (typically numbers) that are indexed with a single integer. A two-dimensional array is a matrix, containing elements indexed by a pair of integers, that is, the row index and the column index. More generally, an *n*-dimensional array is a set of elements with the same data type that are indexed by a tuple of *n* integers.

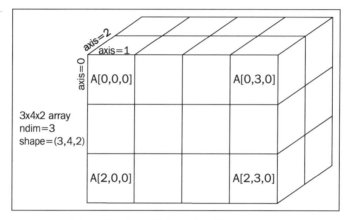

Schematic of a multidimensional NumPy array

All elements in an array must have the same type: it is called the **data type** (dtype). There are multiple possible types in NumPy: Booleans, signed/unsigned integers, single-precision/double-precision floating point numbers, complex numbers, strings, and so on. Custom data types can also be defined.

Elements in an array are stored internally in a contiguous block of memory. For example, the elements in a vector of size 10 possess 10 consecutive memory addresses. When the dimension of the array is two or more, there is more than a unique choice for the ordering of the elements. For a matrix, the elements can be stored in **row-major order** (also known as **C-order**) or **column-major order** (also known as **Fortran-order**), depending on which index among the horizontal or vertical indexes moves the fastest as one goes along all elements in the array. This notion generalizes in three or more dimensions. The default order in NumPy is the C-order, but that can be changed when creating an array, typically with the order keyword argument.

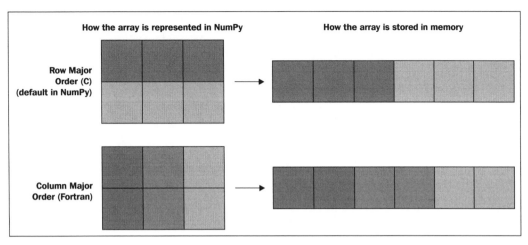

Difference between row-major and column-major order in multidimensional arrays

This notion can be extended to any number of dimensions. The **stride** defines the number of steps in each dimension that are made as one goes through all elements. NumPy handles all these low-level details automatically and provides convenient ways of creating, manipulating, and computing on these arrays. Most of the time, we do not need to bother about these details and we can think about our variables as multidimensional arrays. However, knowing how things work internally allows us to fix certain bugs and to optimize some portions of the code that involve very large arrays.

The advantage of arrays compared with native Python types is that it is possible to perform very efficient computations on arrays instead of relying on Python loops. The difference is that the loop is implemented internally in C by NumPy instead of Python, so that there is no longer the cost of interpretation within the loop. Indeed, Python being an interpreted, dynamically-typed language, each iteration involves various low-level operations performed by Python (type checking and so on). Those operations generally take negligible time, but they become noxious to performance when they are repeated millions of times.

In addition, modern CPUs implement vectorized instructions (SSE, AVX, XOP, and so on) that use large registers (128 bits or 256 bits) and can contain several single-precision or double-precision floating points. If NumPy is compiled with the adequate options, array computations can benefit from these vectorized CPU instructions and can be more than two or four times faster.

These are the main reasons why vectorized computations with NumPy can potentially be much more efficient than Python loops. One refers to the **Single Instruction, Multiple Data (SIMD)** paradigm of computation, since the same computation is performed on multiple items in an array operation with NumPy. We will demonstrate this with the help of our previous example.

Reimplementing the example with arrays

Let's rewrite our example using arrays. First, we need to import NumPy. In IPython, we can use the `%pylab` magic command (or start IPython with `ipython --pylab`), which loads NumPy and Matplotlib within the interactive namespace (available as `np` for `numpy` and `plt` for `matplotlib.pyplot`). It is the most convenient way of using NumPy in an IPython interactive session. The other possibility is to import NumPy with `import numpy` (or `import numpy as np` for the lazy ones) or `from numpy import *`. The former syntax is to be preferred in a script, while the latter can be used in an interactive session. Here, and in all the following chapters, we will always assume that the `pylab` mode has been activated as follows:

```
In [1]: %pylab
```

First, we need to generate some random data. NumPy provides an efficient way of doing this as shown in the following command:

```
In [2]: positions = rand(10000000,2)
```

The `positions` array is a two-dimensional array with 10 million rows and two columns containing independent uniform random numbers between zero and one. We note that we do not use a `for` loop for the array creation. Loops should be avoided every time it is possible to use a NumPy operation instead. Let's look at some properties of this object as follows:

```
In [3]: type(positions)
Out[3]: numpy.ndarray
In [4]: positions.ndim, positions.shape
Out[4]: 2, (10000000, 2)
```

The `shape` attribute contains the array shape as a tuple of integers. Other important attributes of an array include:

- `ndim`: The number of dimensions, which is also `len(positions.shape)`
- `size`: The total number of elements (the product of all values in `positions.shape`)
- `itemsize`: The size in bytes of each element (four for an `int32` data type, eight for `float64`, and so on)

Now, we will compute the squared distance of each position to our position of interest in two steps. We first enter the following command:

```
In [5]: x, y = positions[:,0], positions[:,1]
```

Here, x and y contain the *x* and *y* coordinates of all positions. Indeed, the variable positions[:,0] refers to the first column of positions (indexing is zero-based in Python). This is a special Python/NumPy syntax for indexing. The brackets [] allow to access elements from a Python-container object. Inside the brackets, the notation :,0 refers to all pairs of indices with any first element (the colon :) and a second element equal to zero. Since, in NumPy, the first dimension always refers to the row and the second dimension to the column, we are precisely referring to the first column here. Similarly, positions[:,1] refers to the second column, with the *y* coordinates of all positions. The variables x and y are one-dimensional vectors. Let's compute the distances variable with the following command:

```
In [6]: distances = (x - .5) ** 2 + (y - .5) ** 2
```

Here, we compute the vector of distances from the position of interest (0.5, 0.5) to all positions. Indeed, the x - .5 expression subtracts 0.5 from all elements in the first column of positions. The reason is that x is a one-dimensional vector with 10 million elements, and 0.5 is simply a floating point number. The convention in NumPy follows the mathematical convention in vector calculus, that is, the subtraction is performed on all elements in the array.

In the same way, (x - .5) ** 2 computes the square of all elements in the vector appearing inside the parentheses. Finally, the + operator performs the point-wise operations of two 10 million-long vectors.

We see that NumPy allows to perform vector operations with a really simple syntax. Computing with arrays is a very specific way of programming and requires some time to master. It is quite different to the standard sequential way of programming in most languages, but it is far more efficient in Python, as we can see in the following commands:

```
In [7]: %timeit exec(In[6])
1 loops, best of 3: 508 ms per loop
```

When computing the distances variable again with the %timeit magic function, we find that the computation is much faster than the pure Python version. Even if we add the computation of the smallest element, which is also easy with NumPy, we still find a total time that is *30 times faster than the pure Python version*, as shown in the following commands:

```
In [8]: %timeit ibest = distances.argmin()
1 loops, best of 3: 20 ms per loop
```

In conclusion, the *raison d'être* of multidimensional arrays is to avoid Python loops as much as possible when performing numerical computations on large amounts of data. Vectorizing computations in an algorithm can sometimes be difficult, but it is always worth it in terms of performance improvement.

Creating and loading arrays

In this section, we will see how we can create and load arrays either from scratch or from existing data. This is the first step when analyzing data with Python.

Creating arrays

There are several ways of creating an array. We will review them in this section.

From scratch, element by element

First, we can create an array by manually specifying its coefficients. This is the most direct way of creating an array, but it is not used very often in practice. The NumPy function `array` takes a list of elements and returns a corresponding NumPy array, as shown in the following example (the `pylab` mode of IPython needs to be activated):

```
In [1]: x = array([1, 2, 3])
In [2]: x.shape
Out[2]: (3,)
In [3]: x.dtype
Out[3]: dtype('int32')
```

Here, we create a one-dimensional array (that is, a vector) with three 32-bit integers (the default type of integers on 32-bit systems). The data type of the created array is automatically inferred from the elements provided in `array`. We can force the data type with the `dtype` keyword argument as follows:

```
In [4]: x = array([1, 2, 3], dtype=float64)
In [5]: x.dtype
Out[5]: dtype('float64')
```

To create two-dimensional arrays (matrices), we need to provide a nested list of lists, each inner list containing one row, as follows:

```
In [6]: array([[1, 2, 3], [4, 5, 6]])
Out[6]:
array([[1, 2, 3],
       [4, 5, 6]])
```

To create an *n*-dimensional array, we need to provide a nested list of lists of lists with *n* levels of recursion. For example, let's create a multiplication table using two nested Python lists comprehensions:

```
def mul1(n):
    return array([[(i + 1) * (j + 1) for i in xrange(n)] for j in
xrange(n)])
```

This function takes the table size as a parameter, and creates the multiplication table as an array from a list of rows, as shown in the following example:

```
In [7]: mul1(4)
Out[7]:
array([[ 1,  2,  3,  4],
       [ 2,  4,  6,  8],
       [ 3,  6,  9, 12],
       [ 4,  8, 12, 16]])
In [8]: %timeit mul1(100)
100 loops, best of 3: 5.14 ms per loop
```

We will see later more efficient ways of creating this multiplication table.

From scratch, using predefined templates

Creating arrays by specifying the individual coefficients manually is rarely practical. One can use any of the several convenient functions defined in NumPy to create typical arrays with the desired shape. For example, to create a vector filled with 100 zeros, we can use the following command:

```
In [1]: x = zeros(100)
```

To create a 2D matrix, we need to provide a tuple with the desired shape as an argument, hence the double parentheses in the following command:

```
In [2]: x = zeros((10, 10))
```

The default data type is `float64`. Similarly, the `ones` function creates an array filled with the value 1. The functions `identity`, `eye`, and `diag` allow to create diagonal matrices.

There are also several convenient functions that create vectors with regularly spaced numbers, as shown in the following example:

```
In [5]: arange(2, 10, 2)
Out[5]:
array([2, 4, 6, 8])
```

Here, we create a vector of numbers linearly spaced between 2 and 10 with a step of two. Note that the first number is *included* (the first 2), but the last number in the sequence (10) is *excluded*. This is a general convention in Python that is actually more intuitive than what it looks like. Another related function is linspace, which is similar to arange, except that the *size* of the output vector, and not the step, is provided as a third argument. This time, the first and last elements of the sequence are included.

Function signatures

The function signatures, including the parameter order and the list of keyword arguments, can be obtained in IPython with ? or help(). In addition, in the Qt console and in the notebook, typing linspace(will automatically open a tooltip with linspace(function's signature. The tooltip can then be expanded by pressing *Tab*.

From random values

NumPy provides various random sampling routines for generating arrays with independent random values following different probability distributions. For example, to create a 2 x 5 array with random floating numbers uniformly sampled between 0 and 1, we can use the rand function as follows:

```
In [1]: rand(2, 5)
Out[1]:
array([[ 0.925,  0.849,  0.858,  0.269,  0.644],
       [ 0.796,  0.001,  0.183,  0.397,  0.788]])
```

Notice the absence of double parentheses when specifying the shape of the array in rand (NumPy oddity).

Number formatting in IPython

The way numbers are displayed in IPython can be specified with the %precision magic command. For example, to display exactly three decimals for floating point numbers, we can type %precision 3 in IPython. Actually, any formatting string can be provided, as explained in the documentation %precision?.

Other functions include randn (random values sampled from a Gaussian distribution), randint (random integers), exponential (exponential distribution), and so on. Related functions include shuffle and permutation, which randomly permute existing arrays.

Loading arrays

The main interest of the array structure is the possibility to load existing data from Python or from an external source. NumPy provides efficient and convenient ways of loading multidimensional arrays from text (Python strings or text/CSV files) or from binary buffers or files. In addition, the Pandas package is particularly useful when loading tabular data, that is, tables that contain heterogeneous data types instead of just numbers.

From a native Python object

It is quite common to have data in some native Python object and to want to convert it into a NumPy array. The standard method is to use the array function. When we created arrays by directly specifying their values, we actually converted Python lists of numbers into arrays.

From a buffer or an external file

Another common way of creating an array is to load data from a memory buffer or from a file, with either binary or string elements. From a Python buffer object, which we know the exact data type of, we can obtain a NumPy array with the function frombuffer. Similarly, the fromstring function accepts either ASCII text with values separated by any delimiter or binary data in any data type, as shown in the following example:

```
In [1]: np.fromstring('1 2 5 10', dtype=int, sep=' ')
Out[1]: array([ 1,   2,   5, 10])
```

The functions fromfile, loadtxt, and genfromtxt allow to load data from text files or binary files and convert them into NumPy arrays. The function loadtxt is a simplified version of genfromtxt, useful when the file format is straightforward. The fromfile function is highly efficient with binary data. For example, to import data contained in the text files of the Facebook dataset, we can enter the following commands:

```
In [1]: cd fbdata
In [2]: loadtxt('0.edges')
Out[2]:
array([[ 236.,   186.],
       ...,
       [ 291.,   339.]])
```

Finally, saving arrays in files is as easy as loading NumPy arrays. There are basically two functions, `save` and `savetxt`, which save an array into a binary and text file, respectively. Relatedly, the `loadz` and `savez` functions are also conveniently used to save *dictionaries* of variables of any type (including NumPy arrays). All these functions use platform-independent file formats.

Using Pandas

Pandas is another, more recent Python package that provides convenient and efficient ways of loading and manipulating data sets from heterogeneous sources. It is particularly useful when dealing with tabular data sets, in opposition to purely numerical data (matrices or arrays of numbers). It can handle missing values and data alignment issues (for example, with time series). The loaded data sets can be used with NumPy for efficient numerical computations. In brief, Pandas provides high-level access to tabular data, whereas NumPy provides lower-level access to raw homogeneous multidimensional arrays.

The future of NumPy

Travis Oliphant, the creator of NumPy, is currently working on its successor, Blaze. This project will unify many of the features currently offered by NumPy, Pandas, SciPy, Numba, Theano, and so on within a single framework.

Here is an example of how we can load a data set with Pandas. We will download and analyze a data set about a large number of cities around the world and their population. This data set has been created by **MaxMind** and is available for free from `http://www.maxmind.com`.

Online public data sets

With the open data movement, more and more data is becoming publicly available. Analyzing interesting data is a good way to gain experience with the tools described in this book, which are particularly well adapted for this task. However, it is not always obvious to find good data sets online. The following are some links containing pointers to high quality data sets, often maintained by government agencies, international organizations, universities, or research institutes, and so on:

- Research-quality data sets, maintained by Hilary Mason, are available at `https://bitly.com/bundles/hmason/1`.
- Public data, maintained by Google, is available at `http://www.google.com/publicdata/`.
- Data catalogs are available at `http://datacatalogs.org/dataset`.

We first download the ZIP file and uncompress it in a folder, as shown in the following commands (the ZIP file is about 40 MB large, so downloading it may take a while):

```
In [1]: import urllib2, zipfile
In [2]: url = 'http://ipython.rossant.net/'
In [3]: filename = 'cities.zip'
In [4]: downloaded = urllib2.urlopen(url + filename)
In [5]: folder = 'data'
In [6]: mkdir $folder
In [7]: with open(filename, 'wb') as f:
            f.write(downloaded.read())
In [8]: with zipfile.ZipFile(filename) as zip:
            zip.extractall(folder)
```

For convenience, we can create an alias to the newly-created folder with the command %bookmark citiesdata data. Now, we are going to load the CSV file that has been extracted with Pandas. The read_csv function of Pandas can open any CSV file, as shown in the following commands:

```
In [9]: import pandas as pd
In [10]: filename = 'data/worldcitiespop.txt'
In [11]: data = pd.read_csv(filename)
```

Now, let's explore the newly created data object:

```
In [12]: type(data)
Out[12]: pandas.core.frame.DataFrame
```

The data object is a DataFrame object, a Pandas type consisting of a two-dimensional labeled data structure with columns of potentially different types (like an Excel spreadsheet). Like a NumPy array, the shape attribute returns the shape of the table. But unlike NumPy, the DataFrame object has a richer structure, and, in particular, the keys method returns the names of the different columns, as shown in the following commands:

```
In [13]: data.shape, data.keys()
Out[13]: ((3173958, 7),
  Index([Country, City, AccentCity, Region, Population, Latitude,
Longitude], dtype=object))
```

We can see that `data` has more than three million lines and seven columns including the country, city, population, and geographical coordinates of each city. The `head` and `tail` methods allow to take a quick look at the beginning and the end of the table respectively. Note that, when using Pandas from the IPython notebook, the displayed data can be formatted as an HTML table for more convenient reading, as shown in the following example:

```
In [14]: data.tail()
```

The following is the example table:

	Country	City	AccentCity	Region	Population	Latitude	Longitude
3173953	zw	zimre park	Zimre Park	4	NaN	-17.866111	31.213611
3173954	zw	ziyakamanas	Ziyakamanas	0	NaN	-18.216667	27.950000
3173955	zw	zizalisari	Zizalisari	4	NaN	-17.758889	31.010556
3173956	zw	zuzumba	Zuzumba	6	NaN	-20.033333	27.933333
3173957	zw	zvishavane	Zvishavane	7	79876	-20.333333	30.033333

Displaying a Pandas table in the IPython notebook

We can see that some cities have **NaN** (**Not a Number**) values as populations. The reason is that the population is not available for all cities in the data set, and Pandas handles those missing values transparently.

We will see in the next sections what manipulations and computations we can actually perform with this data set to get useful information about it.

Working with arrays

Once NumPy arrays are created or loaded, there are basically three things that we can do with them:

- Selection
- Manipulation
- Computation

Selection

Selection consists of accessing one or several elements within an array. It can be done with NumPy or Pandas.

Using Pandas

Let's continue with our example data opened with Pandas. Each column of the data object of DataFrame can be accessed through its name. In IPython, tab completion proposes the different columns of the data. In the following example, we get the names of all cities (AccentCity is the full name of the city, with uppercase characters and accents):

```
In [15]: data.AccentCity
Out[15]:
0                    Aixas
1                Aixirivali
...
3173956              Zuzumba
3173957            Zvishavane
Name: AccentCity, Length: 3173958
```

This column is an instance of the Series class. We can access certain rows using indexing. In the following example, we get the name of the 30,001th city (remembering that indexing is zero-based):

```
In [16]: data.AccentCity[30000]
Out[16]: 'Howasiyan'
```

So, we can access an element using its index. But how can we obtain a city from its name? For example, we would like to obtain the population and GPS coordinates of New York. A possibility might be to loop through all cities and check their names, but it would be extremely slow because the Python loops on millions of elements are not optimized at all. Pandas and NumPy offer a much more elegant and efficient way called **Boolean indexing**.

There are two steps that typically occur on the same line of code. First, we create an array with Boolean values indicating, for each element, whether it satisfies a condition or not (here, whether the city name is New York). Then, we pass this array of Booleans as an index to our original array. The result is then a subpart of the full array with only the elements corresponding to True, as shown in the following example:

```
In [17]: data[data.AccentCity=='New York']
Out[17]:
         Country     City AccentCity Region  Population    Latitude
Longitude
998166        gb  new york   New York     H7         NaN   53.083333
-0.150000
...
2990572       us  new york   New York     NY     8107916   40.714167
-74.006389
```

The same syntax works in NumPy and Pandas. Here, we find a dozen cities named `New York`, but only one happens to be in the New York state. To access a single element with Pandas, we can use the `.ix` attribute (ix for index) as shown in the following commands:

```
In [18]: ny = 2990572
In [19]: data.ix[ny]
Out[19]:
Country               us
City           new york
AccentCity     New York
Region               NY
Population      8107916
Latitude       40.71417
Longitude      -74.00639
Name: 2990572
```

Using NumPy

Now, let's turn this series object into a pure NumPy array. We go from the Pandas world to NumPy (keeping in mind that Pandas is built on top of NumPy). We will mostly work with the population count of all cities as shown in the following commands:

```
In [20]: population = array(data.Population)
In [21]: population.shape
Out[21]: (3173958,)
```

The `population` array is a one-dimensional vector with the populations of all cities (or NaN if the population is not available). The population of New York can be accessed in NumPy with basic indexing, as follows:

```
In [22]: population[ny]
Out[22]: 8107916.0
```

Let's find out how many cities do have an actual population count. To do this, we will select all elements in the population array that have a value different from NaN. We can use the NumPy function `isnan` as follows:

```
In [23]: isnan(population)
Out[23]: array([ True,   True,   True,  ...,  True,   True,  False],
dtype=bool)
```

```
In [24]: x = population[~_]
In [25]: len(x), len(x) / float(len(population))
Out[25]: (47980, 0.015)
```

Note that `~_` contains the negative values of `isnan(population)`. We find that there are roughly 48,000 cities, corresponding to 1.5 percent of all cities in this data set, which have an actual population count.

More indexing possibilities

More generally, indexing allows us to take any portion of an array. We saw in the previous section how to filter an array with a Boolean condition. We can also specify directly the list of indices we want to keep. For instance, if x is a one-dimensional NumPy array, `x[i:j:k]` represents a view on x with only those elements having indices between i (included) and j (excluded) with a step of k. If i is omitted, it is assumed to be zero. If j is omitted, it is assumed to be the length of the array in that dimension. Negative values mean we count from the end. Finally, the default value for k is one. This notation is also valid in multiple dimensions; for example, `M[i:j,k:l]` creates a submatrix view on a 2D array M. Also, we can use `x[::-1]` to get x in the reverse order.

These conventions, with i included and j excluded, are convenient when working with consecutive portions of an array. For example, the first and second halves of x, assuming a size 2n, are simply `x[:n]` and `x[n:]`. In addition, the length of `x[i:j]` is simply j - i. In the end, there should not be +1 or -1 values hanging around in indices in general.

An important point to consider with array views is that they point to the same location in memory. So a view on a large array does not imply memory allocation, and changing the values of elements in the view also changes the corresponding values in the original array, as shown in the following example:

```
In [1]: x = rand(5)
In [2]: x
Out[2]: array([ 0.5  ,   0.633,   0.158,   0.862,   0.35 ])
In [3]: y = x[::2]
In [4]: y
Out[4]: array([ 0.5  ,   0.158,   0.35 ])
In [5]: y[0] = 1
In [6]: x
Out[6]: array([ 1.  ,   0.633,   0.158,   0.862,   0.35 ])
```

In this example, y contains all elements in x with even indices (here, indices zero, two, and four). Changing the value of y[0] changes both y[0] and x[0], since y[0] refers to the first element of x. If this behavior is unwanted, it is possible to force the creation of a new array with y = x.copy() or y = array(x). In the latter case, it is also possible to change the data type of x, with the dtype keyword argument.

Finally, another way of selecting a portion of an array consists in passing an array with explicit integer values for indices. This is called **fancy indexing**. If x is a one-dimensional vector, and indices is another one-dimensional vector (or a list) with positive integers, then x[indices] returns a vector containing x[indices[0]], x[indices[1]], and so on. Therefore, the length of x[indices] is equal to the length of indices and not the length of x, as shown here:

```
In [7]: ind = [0, 1, 0, 2]
In [8]: x[ind]
Out[8]: array([ 1.   ,  0.633,  1.   ,  0.158])
```

Note that a given index can be repeated several times in the index array.

Manipulation

Arrays can be manipulated and reshaped, which can sometimes be useful when performing vectorized computations. It is also possible to construct a new array from identical copies of an original array. The complete list of routines can be found in the NumPy reference guide at http://docs.scipy.org/doc/numpy/reference/routines.html.

Reshaping

First, the reshape method allows to change the shape of an array if the total number of elements is kept constant, as shown in the following example:

```
In [1]: rand(6)
Out[1]: array([ 0.872,  0.257,  0.083,  0.788,  0.931,  0.232])
In [2]: x.reshape((2, 3))
array([[ 0.872,  0.257,  0.083],
       [ 0.788,  0.931,  0.232]])
```

It is possible to use -1 in at most one dimension in the argument of reshape to specify that its value must be automatically inferred; for example, x.reshape((2, -1)) instead of x.reshape((2, 3)).

The number of dimensions can also be changed with `ravel` (to remove all multidimensional structures in an array and return a flattened vector), `squeeze` (to remove all single-dimensional entries from the shape of an array), and `expand_dims` (to insert a new axis in an array).

Repeating and concatenating

The `tile` and `repeat` functions allow to create copies of an array, either by concatenating identical copies of it along a specified axis, or by copying every coefficient any number of times, as shown in the following example:

```
In [1]: x = arange(3)
In [2]: tile(x, (2, 1))
Out[2]:
array([[0, 1, 2],
       [0, 1, 2]])
In [3]: repeat(x, 2)
Out[3]:
array([0, 0, 1, 1, 2, 2])
```

Here, we first create an array with a vertical stack of two identical copies of x, and we create a new array with each element of x repeated three times. The second argument of repeat can also be a list `reps`, in which case the coefficient `x[i]` is repeated `reps[i]` times.

For example, let's create a multiplication table using `reshape` and `tile`. The idea is to first define one row vector and one column vector with all integers between 1 and n, tile them, and multiply them, knowing that the multiplication occurs element-wise as shown in the following code snippet:

```
def mul2(n):
    M = arange(1, n + 1).reshape((-1, 1))
    M = tile(M, (1, n))
    N = arange(1, n + 1).reshape((1, -1))
    N = tile(N, (n, 1))
    return M * N
```

Let's time the execution of this function using the following commands:

```
In [1]: %timeit mul2(100)
10000 loops, best of 3: 188 us per loop
```

This function is about 27 times faster than the previous version `mul1`, which used nested Python loops.

Also, we can use `hstack`, `vstack`, `dstack`, or `concatenate` to join several arrays into a single array along the first, second, third, or any dimension, respectively.

Similarly, the `hsplit`, `vsplit`, `dsplit`, or `split` functions allow to split an array into several consecutive subarrays along any dimension, as shown in the following example:

```
In [1]: x = arange(6)
In [2]: split(x, 2)
Out[2]:
[array([0, 1, 2]), array([3, 4, 5])]
In [3]: split(x, [2,5])
Out[3]:
[array([0, 1]), array([2, 3, 4]), array([5])]
```

The second argument of `split` is either an integer, n, in which case the array is split into *n* equal arrays, or a list with the indices where the array should be split (that is, the indices of the first element in each subarray except the first).

Broadcasting

In the previous multiplication table example, we had to repeat identical copies of a row and a column so that we could multiply the two arrays with identical shapes (n, n). Actually, the `repeat` step is unnecessary, as arrays with different shapes can still be compatible under specific conditions; this is called **broadcasting**. The general rule is that *two dimensions are compatible when they are equal, or when one of them is 1.* For example, two arrays, M and N, of the shape (1, n) and (n, 1) can be multiplied together, because in the first dimension, M array's shape is 1, whereas N array's shape is 1 in the second dimension. The dimension equal to one is transparently and silently stretched to match the other dimension, and this operation does not involve memory copy.

Therefore, we can get rid of the `tile` operation in the multiplication table example as follows:

```
def mul3(n):
    M = arange(1, n + 1).reshape((-1, 1))
    N = arange(1, n + 1).reshape((1, -1))
    return M * N
```

The following commands are used:

```
In [1]: timeit mul3(100)
10000 loops, best of 3: 71.8 us per loop
```

Finally, `mul3` is about 2.6 times faster than `mul2`, and about 70 times faster than `mul1`! The reason is that `tile` involves array copying and memory allocation, whereas only multiplications happen in `mul3`.

Permuting

Several functions allow to permute the axes in an array. For example, the `transpose` function permutes the dimensions of an array. The indices describing the permutation can be provided in the `axes` keyword argument.

Other transposition functions that may be useful include `fliplr` and `flipud` to flip an array in the left/right or up/down direction, `roll` to perform a circular permutation of the elements along a given axis, and `rot90` to rotate an array by 90 degrees in the counter-clockwise direction.

Computation

The whole point of creating and manipulating arrays is to perform efficient vectorized computations with them. The four elementary operations work between arrays under the condition that they have compatible shapes. In addition, a lot of mathematical functions are available in the vectorized form for NumPy arrays.

If `A` and `B` are two NumPy arrays with compatible shapes, `A + B`, `A - B`, `A x B`, and `A / B` are element-wise operations. In particular, when `A` and `B` are two-dimensional matrices, `A x B` is *not* the matrix product. The matrix product is rather provided by the `dot` function, which more generally computes the dot product of two arrays.

Common unary operations include `-A`, `A ** x` (coefficients to power x), `abs(A)` (absolute value), `sign(A)` (an array with `-1`, `0`, or `1` depending on the sign of each element), `floor(A)` (floor of each element), `sqrt(A)` (square root), `log(A)` (natural logarithm), `exp(A)` (exponential), and a lot of other mathematical functions (trigonometric, hyperbolic, arithmetic functions, and so on).

NumPy also provides functions to compute the sum (`sum`) or product (`prod`) of all elements in an array or in a given dimension. The `axis` keyword argument specifies the dimensions on which the sum is to be performed. This function returns an array with one dimension less than the original array.

The max and min functions return the largest and lowest values in an array or in a given dimension. The argmin and argmax functions return the index of the smallest or largest element of the array. For example, continuing with our cities example we can have the following commands for the locate function:

```
In [26]: def locate(x, y):
             # locations is a Ncities x 2 array with the cities positions
             locations = data[['Latitude','Longitude']].as_matrix()
             d = locations - array([x, y])
             # squared distances from every city to the position (x,y)
             distances = d[:,0] ** 2 + d[:,1] ** 2
             # closest in the index of the city achieving the minimum
distance to the position (x,y)
             closest = distances.argmin()
             # we return the name of that city
             return data.AccentCity[closest]
In [27]: print(locate(48.861, 2.3358))
Paris
```

The locate function takes two coordinates with a position's latitude and longitude, and returns the closest city's name. The argmin function returns the index of the city with the smallest distance to the specified position.

Finally, statistical functions such as mean, median, std, and var compute the mean, median, standard deviation, and variance of the elements along a given dimension or across the whole array. Also, the describe method of Pandas objects gives several useful statistics (including the mean, standard deviation, the 50 percent quantile or median, and the 25 precent and 75 percent quantiles) as follows:

```
In [28]: population.describe()
count        47980.000000
mean         47719.570634
std         302888.715626
min              7.000000
25%           3732.000000
50%          10779.000000
75%          27990.500000
max       31480498.000000
```

Related functions that can be useful when simulating mathematical models include diff (discrete difference), cumsum (cumulative sum), and cumprod (cumulative product). The diff function allows to compute a discrete *derivative* of a signal (up to a scalar coefficient), whereas cumsum computes a discrete *indefinite integral* of a signal.

Advanced mathematical processing

NumPy provides all necessary types and routines for doing efficient numerical computations with Python. SciPy is built on top of NumPy and implements a large variety of higher-level mathematical processing algorithms. These algorithms span several areas of numerical computing, such as optimization, linear algebra, signal processing, statistics, and the like. Also, the various **SciKits** packages (scikit-learn, scikit-image, and so on) are yet more advanced packages implementing highly specialized algorithms in specific domains (machine learning, image processing, and so on).

We give here a short overview of the scientific computing features provided by SciPy and a few other packages. The full list of features can be found on the official reference guide: http://docs.scipy.org/doc/scipy/reference/. Giving practical examples and applications is beyond the scope of this book, and the interested reader can find a wide variety of examples in the *NumPy Cookbook, Ivan Idris, Packt Publishing*, and *Learning SciPy for Numerical and Scientific Computing, Francisco Blanco-Silva, Packt Publishing*, both by Packt Publishing.

- **Linear algebra** routines are provided by the scipy.linalg subpackage: solvers of linear equations, matrix routines, eigenvalue problems, matrix decomposition, and so on.

- **Optimization routines** are provided by the scipy.optimize subpackage: unconstrained or constrained minimization of real-valued functions, global optimization, curve fitting, and so on.

- **Numerical integrators** are provided by the scipy.integrate subpackage. It can be used to solve differential equations, for example, in physics simulation engines.

- **Signal processing** algorithms are implemented in the scipy.signal subpackage: convolutions, linear filters, wavelets, and so on. The scipy.fftpack subpackage, which implements Fourier transforms routines, and the scipy.ndimage subpackage, which implements several image processing algorithms. Finally, other image processing packages of interest include scikit-image, PIL, and OpenCV (computer vision).

- **Statistical routines** are provided by the `scipy.stats` subpackage: probability distributions, descriptive statistics and statistical tests, and so on. `SciPy.cluster` implements clustering algorithms that can be useful to find categories in unstructured data. Other statistical packages of interest include `Pandas` and `scikit-learn` (machine learning).

Summary

In this chapter, we described the multidimensional array object offered by NumPy, and we showed how it can be used for efficient computations on numerical data sets. In particular, it is well adapted for loading any sort of data, and the Pandas package makes this task straightforward, even with complex data files. Using advanced algorithms is possible with IPython with the help of powerful external packages, such as NumPy, SciPy, and the SciKit libraries. However, this subject is beyond the scope of this book, and the interested reader can find a variety of examples in the *NumPy Cookbook, Ivan Idris, Packt Publishing* and *Learning SciPy for Numerical and Scientific Computing, Francisco Blanco-Silva, Packt Publishing*.

In the next chapter, we will present the visualization-related possibilities offered by IPython and Matplotlib, which are very often used in conjunction with NumPy for interactive visualization of data.

4
Interactive Plotting and Graphical Interfaces

In this chapter, we will show the graphical capabilities of Python and how they can be used interactively with IPython.

NumPy provides a very efficient way of dealing with large amounts of data structured as multidimensional arrays. But looking at grids of numbers is often much less intuitive than looking at plots, such as curves, scatter plots, images, and likewise. Matplotlib is a particularly rich Python package for generating high-quality figures from NumPy data. It provides a simple, high-level interface much similar to Matlab, a commercial product that is popular in the engineering and scientific worlds. Matplotlib integrates very well with IPython.

We will also introduce **Graphical User Interface (GUI)** programming. Covering this rich subject extensively is far beyond the scope of this book. So we will only see basic examples in this chapter. We will cover the following points:

- Plotting figures with Matplotlib
- Image processing techniques
- Geographical maps
- Introduction to Graphical User Interfaces
- Designing and debugging GUIs with IPython's event loop integration

Figures with Matplotlib

There are a lot of Python packages for curve plotting, but the most widely used one, by far, is Matplotlib. It is one of the most complete and powerful graphical libraries. It can be used both for interactive visualization and for generating high-quality figures that can be readily used in scientific publications. In addition, its high-level interface makes it particularly easy to use.

In this section, we will show some of the possibilities offered by Matplotlib as well as how it can be advantageously used with IPython.

Setting up IPython for interactive visualization

IPython implements a loop integration system that allows to display graphical windows from the command-line interface without blocking the console. This is very useful when using Matplotlib or when creating graphical user interfaces.

Using Matplotlib

Figures can be displayed interactively in IPython using event loop integration. Then, they can be updated dynamically from the command-line interface. The `%pylab` magic command (or the `--pylab` option to the `ipython` shell command) activates this integration automatically. It is possible to choose the backend renderer used for Matplotlib and IPython, for example, `--pylab qt`, which requires PyQt or PySide.

We will assume that the `%pylab` mode is active in IPython throughout this chapter. When using Matplotlib from a script instead from IPython, we can put the `from pylab import *` command at the top of the script. In a Python module, it might be a better idea to use `import matplotlib.pyplot as plt` so that the Matplotlib objects stay within their namespace.

Also, the way of generating plots is slightly different in a script compared to IPython. In a script, the figure is displayed only when the function `show()` is called, typically, at the very end of the script, whereas, in the IPython command-line interface, the figure is shown and updated at each plot function.

Interactive navigation

When showing a figure with Matplotlib, the window contains a few buttons for navigating interactively within the figure (panning and zooming) and for changing the figure's options. There is also the possibility to save the figure in a bitmap or vector format.

Matplotlib in the IPython notebook

Matplotlib can also be used in the notebook. When launching the notebook with `ipython notebook --pylab inline`, the plots appear in the output cells as images and are saved as base64 strings within the IPYNB files. Without this inline option, figures are displayed in separate windows as usual. It is also possible to activate this option within the notebook by using the command `%pylab inline`.

Standard plots

In this section, we will see some examples of standard plots, such as lines, curves, scatter plots, and bar plots. In the next sections, we will also see images and maps. But Matplotlib offers far more plot types than what we will cover here, including 3D plots, geometrical shapes, vector fields, and so on.

Curves

Drawing a curve with Matplotlib actually means drawing small, successive line segments that give the illusion of a smooth curve when the number of lines is large enough. To plot a mathematical function, one plots samples of this function within a given interval just as NumPy represents functions as arrays with sampled values.

For example, a time-dependent signal can be represented as a one-dimensional vector of sampled values at regular time intervals (for example, every 1 millisecond at a 1 kHz sampling frequency), such that one second of signal is represented as a 1000-unit long vector. The function `plot` can be used to draw this signal on the screen, for example:

```
In [1]:  y = randn(1000)

In [2]:  plot(y)

Out[2]:  [<matplotlib.lines.Line2D at 0x4cf4cf0>]
```

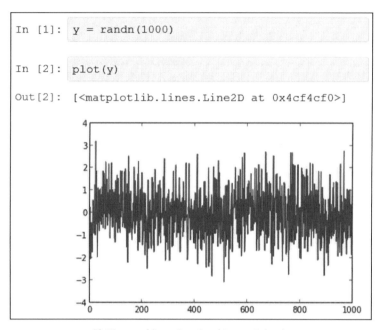

Plotting a white noise signal in a notebook

Here, we generate a vector with random values following independent normal random variables. The resulting signal is a so-called white noise signal, a random signal with a flat power spectral density. When plotting the figure in the notebook with the `--pylab inline` option, Matplotlib generates an image representing this curve, and the image is then automatically inserted in the output cell.

When the `plot` function receives a single vector as an argument, it assumes that this vector contains values on the y axis, whereas values on the x axis are automatically generated as integers from 0 to `len(y)` - 1. To explicitly specify the values on the x axis, we can use the following command: `plot(x,y)`.

Scatter plots

Scatter plots represent sets of points in two dimensions, using pixels or any other marker. Let's continue with our cities example. Assuming we are in the right directory (the `citiesdata` alias), we can load the data and try to plot the geographical coordinates of all the cities:

```
In [1]: import pandas as pd
In [2]: cd citiesdata
In [3]: filename = 'worldcitiespop.txt'
In [4]: data = pd.read_csv(filename)
In [5]: plot(data.Longitude, data.Latitude, ',')
```

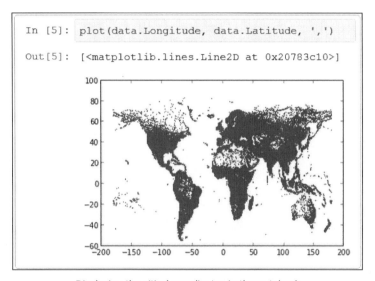

Displaying the cities' coordinates in the notebook

In this example, we plot the latitude (y axis) versus the longitude (x axis) of all the cities. The third argument (`','`) of the `plot` function specifies the marker type. Here, it corresponds to a scatter plot where each city is represented by a single pixel. We can easily recognize the shape of the continents even if they seem a bit distorted. This is because we plot the geographical coordinates in a Cartesian system, whereas it would be more appropriate to use a map projection method. We will get back to this issue later in this chapter.

Bar graphs

A bar graph is typically used for histograms, representing the distribution of values at different intervals. The `hist` function in Matplotlib accepts a vector of values and plots a histogram. The `bins` keyword allows to specify either the number of bins or the list of bins.

For example, let's plot the histogram of the nodes' degrees in the Facebook graph example:

```
In [1]: cd fbdata
In [2]: import networkx as nx
In [3]: g = nx.read_edgelist('0.edges')
In [4]: hist(g.degree().values(), bins=20)
```

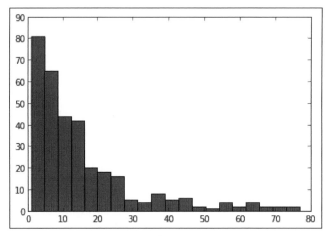

Distribution of the nodes' degrees in a graph

Here, `g.degree()` is a dictionary with the degree of each node (that is, the number of other nodes connected to it). The `values` method returns the list of all the degrees.

There are far more graph types in Matplotlib than what we showed here, and the plotting possibilities are nearly endless. A wide variety of figure examples can be found in the Matplotlib Gallery on the official website (http://matplotlib.org/gallery.html) and in Nicolas Rougier's tutorial (http://www.loria.fr/~rougier/teaching/matplotlib/).

Plot customization

Matplotlib offers a lot of customization options. Here, we will see how to change styles and colors in figures, how to configure axes and legends, and how to display several plots on the same figure.

Styles and colors

By default, curves are continuous and have a uniform color. The style and color of the curves can easily be specified in the `plot` function.

The third argument of the `plot` function specifies the style and color of the curve in a short syntax. For example, `'-r'` means "continuous and red" while `'--g'` means "dashed and green". There are dozens of possible styles such as, `':'` for dotted lines, `'-.'` for dash-dot, `'.'` for points, `','` for pixels, `'o'` for circle markers, and so on.

Also, there are eight colors with a single-character shortcut, namely b, g, and r (primary additive colors — blue, greed, and red); c, m, and y (secondary additive colors — cyan, magenta, and yellow); and k and w (black and white). Any other color can be specified by its hexadecimal code, RGB or RGBA tuple (values between 0 and 1), and so on.

Using a string for specifying the style and color is only a shortcut to the more general way of specifying styles and colors of plots, which is to use particular keyword arguments. These arguments include `linestyle` (or `ls`), `linewidth` (or `lw`), `marker`, `markerfacecolor` (or `mfc`), `markersize` (or `ms`), and so on. The full list of options can be found in the reference documentation of Matplotlib.

Also, when displaying several plots on the same figure, the color of each plot cycles through a predefined set of colors, such as blue, green, red, and so on. This cycle can be customized:

```
In [1]: rcParams['axes.color_cycle'] = ['r', 'k', 'c']
```

Customizing Matplotlib

`rcParams` is a global, dictionary-like variable in Matplotlib with custom parameters. Nearly every aspect of Matplotlib can be configured here. Also, it is possible to specify permanent custom options by saving them in an ASCII text file called `matplotlibrc`, which can be stored either in the current directory (for local options) or in `~/.matplotlib` (for global options). In this file, each line contains a custom parameter, for example, `axes.color_cycle: ['r', 'k', 'c']`.

Grid, axes, and legends

A graph would not convey anything useful about the data without legends and axes. By default, Matplotlib displays axes and ticks automatically. The exact positions of the ticks can be set with `xticks` and `yticks`, and a grid can be added with the `grid` function. The extent of the x and y coordinates can be specified with `xlim` and `ylim`. The axes labels can be set with `xlabel` and `ylabel`. Also, it is possible to specify the legend with the `legend` keyword; the label of each line corresponds to the `label` keyword argument of the `plot` function. Finally, the `title` command displays the name of the figure. The following example illustrates how to use these options:

```
plot(x, sin(x), '-r', label='sinus')
plot(x, cos(x), '--g', label='cosinus')
xticks([-10, 0, 10])
yticks([-1, 0, 1])
ylim(-2, 2)
legend()
grid()
```

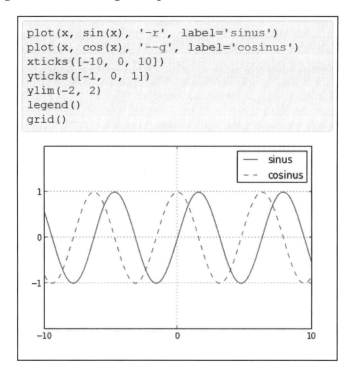

Sine and cosine functions with axes and legends

Superposition of plots

Calling different plot functions updates the same figure in Matplotlib. This is how several plots can be shown on the same figure. To create a new figure in a new window, we need to call the function figure(). Finally, it is possible to display several independent figures within the same window using subplots, as we will see later in this section.

Interaction from IPython

Creating Matplotlib figures with the IPython console using event loop integration allows to interact with them programmatically. It is possible to add new plots in a figure or to update it in real time, as shown in the following example:

```
In [1]: plot(randn(1000, 2))
Out[1]: [<matplotlib.lines.Line2D at 0x4cf4310>,
         <matplotlib.lines.Line2D at 0x4cf4450>]
```

We first create a figure with two white noise signals (the plot function displays every column as an independent curve). Once the window with the figure has opened, we can return to the IPython console without closing that window. The output Out[1] contains a list of Line2D objects. Indeed, Matplotlib uses an object-oriented description of the figure. Let's retrieve the first object (corresponding to the first curve) as follows:

```
In [2]: line = _[0]
```

Tab completion on the line variable then shows the list of methods that we can use to update the figure. For instance, to change the line color from blue to red, we can type the following command:

```
In [3]: line.set_color('r')
```

The figure is then updated accordingly. It may be necessary to force refresh the figure, for example, by panning or zooming.

Finally, let's mention the **Edit** button in the figure window that offers a GUI for updating some figures' properties.

Drawing multiple plots

Multiple independent plots can be displayed on the same figure. We can define a grid with an arbitrary number of rows and columns and plot figures inside each box. Boxes can even span several rows or columns (using `subplot2grid`). For instance, the following example shows how to plot two figures with different coordinate systems side by side:

```
x = linspace(0, 2 * pi, 1000)
y = 1 + 2 * cos(5 * x)
subplot(1,2,1)
plot(x, y)
subplot(1,2,2, polar=True)
polar(x, y)
```

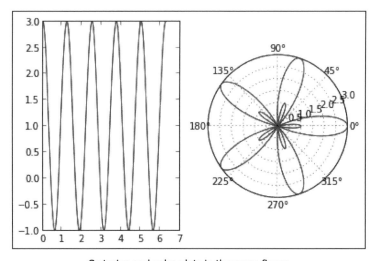

Cartesian and polar plots in the same figure

The `subplot` function simultaneously specifies how many columns (first argument) and rows (second argument) there are, but also the index of the box where the plot will be rendered (third argument, 1-based indexing, from left to right and top to bottom). The `polar=True` keyword argument specifies that the second subplot contains a polar graph. The `polar` function is similar to the `plot` function, but a polar coordinate system containing the attributes theta, and r is used where theta is the angle and r is the radius.

Advanced figures and graphics

In this section, we will show more advanced graphical features offered by Matplotlib that are related to images and maps. We will also take a look at a few other graphical libraries.

Image processing

A colored N x M image can be represented as an N x M x 3 NumPy array corresponding to three N x M matrices for the red, green, and blue channels. Image processing algorithms can then be implemented efficiently with NumPy and SciPy and visualized with Matplotlib. In addition, the PIL package (Python Imaging Library) implements basic image processing routines for pictures.

Loading images

Matplotlib's `imread` function opens a PNG image from the hard drive and returns an N x M x 3 (or N x M x 4 if there is an alpha transparency channel) NumPy array. It can also read other formats if PIL is installed. PIL also offers the `open` function for reading images in any format (BMP, GIF, JPEG, TIFF, and so on).

In the following example, we download a PNG image from a remote URL and load it with `imread`:

```
In [1]: import urllib2
In [2]: png = urllib2.urlopen
('http://ipython.rossant.net/squirrel.png')
In [3]: im = imread(png)
In [4]: im.shape
Out[4]: (300, 300, 3)
```

The `imread` function accepts either an image filename or a Python file-like object (like here, where we use the buffer returned by `urlopen`). The object returned by the `imread` function is a three-dimensional NumPy array.

We can also use PIL for reading images. We can either use `Image.open` to open an image file directly, or we can convert a NumPy array into a PIL image with the `Image.fromarray` function, as follows:

```
In [5]: from PIL import Image
In [6]: img = Image.fromarray((im * 255).astype('uint8'))
```

The `fromarray` function accepts an array with unsigned 8-bit integers, with values between 0 and 255. This is the reason why we need to convert the NumPy array with floating point values to the required data type. Conversely, to convert a PIL image into a NumPy array, we can use the `array` function `im = array(img)`.

Showing images

The `imshow` function of Matplotlib displays an image from a NumPy array, as shown in the following example:

```
In [7]: imshow(im)
```

Displaying an image in the notebook with Matplotlib

The `imshow` function also accepts two-dimensional NumPy arrays (grayscale images). The mapping from scalar values between 0 and 1 to actual pixel colors can be specified with the color map. A color map is a linear gradient of colors defining the color of any value between 0 and 1. A lot of predefined color maps are available in Matplotlib, and the full list can be found here: `http://www.scipy.org/Cookbook/Matplotlib/Show_colormaps`

To specify the color map in `imshow`, we can use the `cmap=get_cmap(name)` keyword argument, where name is the color map's name.

Using PIL

Basic image processing routines, such as rotate, crop, filtering, copy and paste, geometrical transforms, and likewise, are provided by PIL. For example, to rotate an image, we can use the following command:

```
In [9]: imshow(array(img.rotate(45.)))
```

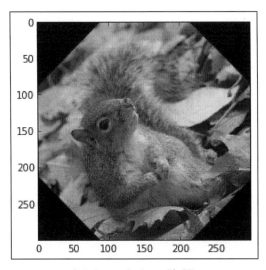

Rotating an image with PIL

Here, we rotate the image 45 degrees counterclockwise, and we convert back the image from PIL to NumPy to display it.

Advanced image processing – color quantization

PIL provides basic image processing functions, whereas SciPy can be used for more advanced algorithms.

Here we will show a small example of an advanced image processing algorithm called color quantization. The principle of this algorithm is to reduce the number of colors of an image while keeping most of the visual structure of the image. In this example, we will implement this algorithm with the `scipy.cluster` package. We will use the k-means algorithm to group the color values into a small number of clusters, and we will assign each pixel to its group's color. Here is the code:

```
In [10]: from scipy.cluster.vq import *
         M = im[:,:,0].ravel()
         centroids, _ = kmeans(M, 4)
         qnt, _ = vq(M, centroids)
         clustered = centroids[reshape(qnt, (300, 300))]
```

We only take the red channel and flatten the image with the `ravel` function so as to treat all pixels equally (that is, we get a one-dimensional vector instead of a two-dimensional matrix). Then, the `kmeans` function finds the clusters in the color space and returns the centroid colors. Finally, the `vq` function assigns each pixel to its centroid index, and we retrieve the resulting image clustered through fancy indexing of the centroid indices (in `qnt`) by the centroid colors (`centroids`). Since the output of this algorithm is a grayscale image, we need to specify a color map. We will use a set of colors that had its heyday some time ago, as shown here:

```
In [11]: cmap = matplotlib.colors.
ListedColormap([(0,.2,.3),(.85,.1,.13),(.44,.6,.6),
(1.,.9,.65)])

In [12]: imshow(clustered, cmap=cmap)
```

Color quantization with SciPy

Here, the `ListedColormap` function creates a custom color map with a discrete set of colors.

Finally, we can save the resulting image as a PNG file with Matplotlib's `imsave` function, as follows:

```
In [13]: imsave('squirrelama.png', clustered, cmap=cmap)
```

Maps

Maps are a complex but important type of figure. The basemap toolkit (which needs to be installed separately) brings geographical capabilities to Matplotlib. It is highly powerful, and we will only scratch the surface in this section. Specifically, we will continue with our cities example to plot a human density map on a planisphere.

First, we retrieve the locations and populations of the cities as follows:

```
In [6]: locations = data[['Longitude','Latitude']].as_matrix()
In [7]: population = data.Population
```

Next, we initialize a world map by specifying the projection type and map boundaries as follows:

```
In [8]: from mpl_toolkits.basemap import Basemap
In [9]: m = Basemap(projection='mill', llcrnrlat=-65, urcrnrlat=85,
            llcrnrlon=-180, urcrnrlon=180)
```

There are a lot of different ways of projecting the surface of the earth on a plane, and the choice of one projection or another depends on the specific application. Here, we use the Miller cylindrical projection. The other keyword arguments give the latitude and longitude of the lower-left and upper-right corners.

The next step is to generate a two-dimensional image with the world population density. To do this, we will need to project the geographical coordinates of the cities on our map, as shown here:

```
In [10]: x, y = m(locations[:,0],locations[:,1])
```

Calling the function m(long,lat) allows to get the (x,y) coordinates of the geographical positions with longitudes and latitudes. To generate the density map, we will also need the coordinates of the map boundaries, as shown here:

```
In [11]: x0, y0 = m(-180, -65)
In [12]: x1, y1 = m(180, 85)
```

Now, let's generate the density map. We will use the histogram2d function, which returns a two-dimensional histogram from a set of points. Here, each point corresponds to a city. We will also use a weight for each city, which corresponds to its population. Care must be taken for cities that do not have a population; we will set the weight to 1000 for these cities, as follows:

```
In [13]: weights = population.copy()
In [14]: weights[isnan(weights)] = 1000
In [15]: h, _, _ = histogram2d(x, y, weights=weights,
bins=(linspace(x0, x1, 500), linspace(y0, y1, 500)))
```

Now the h variable contains the population count in every small rectangle of a 500 x 500 grid spanning the whole planisphere. To generate a density map, we can apply a Gaussian filter to log(h) (corresponding to a kind of kernel density estimation) using SciPy. Using the logarithm can be useful when the values span several orders of magnitude. We also need to take care of zeros (corresponding to empty zones) because the logarithm of zero is undefined:

```
In [16]: h[h == 0] = 1
In [17]: import scipy.ndimage.filters
In [18]: z = scipy.ndimage.filters.gaussian_filter(log(h.T), 1)
```

The filter is applied to the function log(h.T) because the coordinate system of the h variable is transposed compared to the coordinate system of the map. Also, we use a filtering value of 1 here.

Finally, we display the density map as well as the coast lines, as shown here:

```
In [19]: m.drawcoastlines()
In [20]: m.imshow(z, origin='lower', extent=[x0,x1,y0,y1],
cmap=get_cmap('Reds'))
```

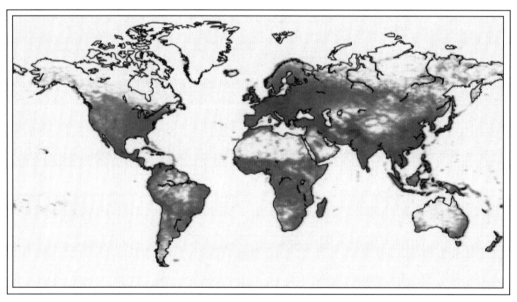

World map with population density using Matplotlib.basemap

3D plots

Matplotlib includes a 3D toolkit called `mplot3d` that can be used for basic 3D plots, such as 3D curves, surface plots, and likewise. As an example, let's create a surface plot. We first need to import the `mplot3d` toolkit as follows:

```
In [1]: from mpl_toolkits.mplot3d import Axes3D
```

Then, we create the x, y, and z coordinates of a surface plot with the following commands:

```
In [2]: # we create a (X, Y) grid
        X = linspace(-5, 5, 50)
        Y = X
        X, Y = meshgrid(X, Y)
        # we compute the Z values
        R = sqrt(X**2 + Y**2)
        Z = sin(R)
```

The NumPy function `meshgrid` returns the coordinates of all the points in a grid that spans a rectangle area defined by the x and y vectors. Finally, we create a 3D canvas and draw the surface plot as follows:

```
In [3]: ax = gca(projection='3d')
        surf = ax.plot_surface(X, Y, Z, rstride=1, cstride=1,
            cmap=mpl.cm.coolwarm, linewidth=0)
```

The Matplotlib function `gca` returns the current axis instance, and we specify here that this instance should use 3D projection. In the `plot_surface` function, the `rstride` and `cstride` keyword arguments give the row and column strides of the surface, whereas `cmap` is the color map and `linewidth` is the width of the wireframe. The following screenshot shows the result:

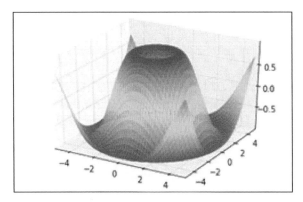

A surface plot with mplot3D

Animations

Matplotlib is capable of creating animations and exporting them as MP4 videos using FFmpeg or MEncoder. The idea is to create a plot and write a function to update it at regular time intervals. The documentation of the animation module can be found at `http://matplotlib.org/api/animation_api.html`. Besides this, a tutorial made by Jake Vanderplas is available at `http://jakevdp.github.com/blog/2012/08/18/matplotlib-animation-tutorial/`.

Other visualization packages

Matplotlib is not the only visualization package in Python. Here are other similar libraries:

- **Chaco**: This is an alternative library to Matplotlib (`http://code.enthought.com/chaco/`)

- **PyQwt**: This is a plotting library based on PyQt (`http://pyqwt.sourceforge.net/`)

- **PyQtGraph**: This package is also based on PyQt and offers 2D and 3D plotting features (`http://www.pyqtgraph.org/`)

- **Visvis**: This package is based on OpenGL; it offers an object-oriented plotting interface (`http://code.google.com/p/visvis/`)

- **Mayavi**: This package offers 3D interactive visualization features, such as curves, surfaces, meshes, volume rendering, and likewise (`http://code.enthought.com/projects/mayavi/`)

- **PyOpenGL**: This Python library gives raw access to the popular OpenGL library; it offers low-level, hardware-accelerated 2D/3D graphics capabilities (`http://pyopengl.sourceforge.net/`)

- **Galry**: This is a high-performance interactive visualization package based on PyOpenGL that targets very large datasets with tens or even hundreds of millions of points (`http://rossant.github.com/galry/`)

Graphical User Interfaces (GUI)

There was a time when human-computer interaction was only done through a command-line interface. Today, most regular computer users are much more confident with a mouse and graphical windows than with a keyboard and black screen with a blinking cursor. For this reason, any developer may be asked at some point to write a graphical interface, even the simplest possible, so as to let non-developer users interact comfortably with the program.

A GUI can easily be integrated in any Python package. There are numerous graphical toolkits for Python, most of them being wrappers to native or C++ graphical libraries. Famous toolkits include Qt, wxWidgets, Tkinter, GTK, and so on. We will use Qt in this book's examples.

GUI programming can be a hard subject, requiring in-depth knowledge of low-level details about the operating system, multithreading programming, as well as some basic notions about human-computer interactions. In this book, we will show a "Hello World" example that gives the very basics of PyQt. We will also see how GUIs can be manipulated interactively with IPython.

Setting up IPython for interactive GUIs

IPython implements a loop integration system that allows the display of graphical windows from the command-line interface without blocking the console. This is very useful when creating GUIs because it becomes possible to interact with the windows dynamically from the command line.

The `%gui` magic command activates the event loop integration. We need to provide the name of the graphical library to use. The possible names are `wx`, `qt`, `gtk`, and `tk`. Here we will work with Qt. So we can type `%gui qt`. The main Qt application is then automatically started in IPython. Another possibility is to launch IPython with `ipython --gui qt`.

The examples in this section require either PyQt4 or PySide. We will assume that PyQt4 is installed, but, if only PySide is installed, it will only be a matter of replacing `PyQt4` with `PySide` in the imports. The Qt binding API provided by both libraries is nearly identical.

A "Hello World" example

In this "Hello World" example, we will show a window with a button triggering a message box. We will also show how to interact with the window from the IPython console.

To define a window, we need to create a class that is derived from the `QWidget` base class. `QWidget` is the base class of all Qt windows and controls, also called widgets. Here is the code of the "Hello World" example:

```
from PyQt4 import QtGui

class HelloWorld(QtGui.QWidget):
    def __init__(self):
        super(HelloWorld, self).__init__()
```

```
        # create the button
        self.button = QtGui.QPushButton('Click me', self)
        self.button.clicked.connect(self.clicked)
        # create the layout
        vbox = QtGui.QVBoxLayout()
        vbox.addWidget(self.button)
        self.setLayout(vbox)
        # show the window
        self.show()

    def clicked(self):
        msg = QtGui.QMessageBox(self)
        msg.setText("Hello World !")
        msg.show()
```

Most of the work happens in the `HelloWorld` widget's constructor. We first need to call the parent constructor. Then, we perform several steps to display the button:

1. We first create a button, as in the instance of the `QPushButton` class. The first argument is the text of the button, and the second one is the parent widget's instance (`self`). Every specific control and widget is defined by a class that is derived from the `QWidget` base class and can be found in the `QtGui` namespace.

2. We define the callback method that is called when the user clicks on the button. The `clicked` attribute is a Qt signal emitted as soon as the user clicks on the button. We connect this signal to the `clicked` method (called a slot) of our `HelloWorld` widget. Signals and slots are Qt's way of making different widgets communicate with each other. Signals are raised when some events occur, and slots connected to these signals are called whenever the signals are raised. Any widget contains a lot of predefined signals. Custom signals can also be created.

3. Then, we need to put the newly created button somewhere on the window. We first need to create a `QVBoxLayout` widget, which is a container widget containing a vertical stack of widgets. Here we only put the button in it, using the `addWidget` method. We also specify that this box is the window's layout. In this way, the main window contains this box that itself contains our button.

4. Finally, we need to show the window with the command `self.show()`.

In the `clicked` method, we create a `QMessageBox` widget representing, by default, a dialog with a text and single **OK** button. The `setText` method specifies the text, and the `show` method displays the window.

Now assuming that the event loop integration with Qt has been activated in IPython either with `%gui qt` or `ipython --gui qt`, we can display the window with the following command:

```
In [1]: window = HelloWorld()
```

The window then appears, and the IPython console is still usable while the window is open.

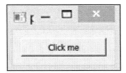

A basic Qt dialog

Clicking on the button shows a dialog containing **Hello World**.

Also, we can interact with the window dynamically from the IPython console. For example, the following command displays the Hello World dialog exactly as if we had clicked on the button:

```
In [2]: window.clicked()
```

This feature is particularly convenient when designing a complex window and for debugging purposes.

Summary

In this chapter, we discovered the graphical possibilities offered by IPython, Matplotlib, and a few other packages. We can create plots, charts, histograms, maps, display and process images, graphical user interfaces, and so on. Figures can also be integrated very easily in a notebook. All aspects of the figures can be customized. These reasons explain why these tools are quite popular in the scientific and engineering communities, where data visualization plays a central role in most applications.

In the next chapter, we will see some techniques to make Python code faster.

5
High-Performance and Parallel Computing

A recurring argument against using Python for high-performance numerical computing is that this language is slow, because it is dynamic and interpreted. A compiled lower-level language such as C can often be orders of magnitude faster. We exposed a first counterargument in *Chapter 3, Numerical Computing with IPython*, with the notion of **vectorization**. Operations on NumPy arrays can be almost as fast as C because slow Python loops are transparently replaced with fast C loops. Sometimes though, it may happen that vectorization is impossible or difficult to implement on some complex algorithms. In these cases, there are fortunately solutions other than throwing away all Python code and coding everything again in C. We will introduce some of these solutions in this chapter.

First, one can take advantage of the multiple cores that are now present in any computer. A standard Python process normally runs on a single core, but it is possible to distribute tasks across multiple cores and even multiple computers in parallel. This is particularly easy to do with IPython. MPI can also be easily used with a few lines of code.

Another popular solution is to first detect the time-critical section of a Python algorithm and then replace it with C code. Typically, only a very small section of the Python code is responsible for most of the algorithm's duration, so that it is possible to keep the rest of the code in Python. **Cython** is an external package which makes this task easier than it sounds: it offers a superset of Python that is compiled and that can be seamlessly integrated within Python code. It is particularly convenient to use it with IPython.

At the end of this chapter, we will have discussed:

* How to distribute independent functions across several cores from IPython
* How to easily use MPI from IPython
* How to convert Python code in C with Cython using a cell magic
* How to use NumPy arrays in Cython for making your code orders of magnitude faster

Interactive task parallelization

In this section, we will see how to distribute tasks across different cores with IPython.

Parallel computing in Python

Python's native support of parallel computing features leaves much to be desired. A long-standing issue is that CPython implements a **Global Interpreter Lock (GIL)**, which, as quoted from the official CPython documentation, is:

> *"...a mutex that prevents multiple native threads from executing Python bytecodes at once."*

The GIL is necessary because CPython's memory management is not thread-safe, but a major drawback is that it can prevent multithreaded CPython programs from taking full advantage of multicore processors.

Python's GIL

The interested reader can find more information about Python's GIL in the following references:

* `http://wiki.python.org/moin/GlobalInterpreterLock`
* `http://www.dabeaz.com/python/UnderstandingGIL.pdf`

Some linear algebraic functions in NumPy may take advantage of multicore processors by releasing the GIL, if NumPy is compiled with the appropriate libraries (ATLAS, MKL, and so on). Otherwise, distributing tasks across different *processes* instead of different *threads* is the typical way of doing parallel computing with Python. As processes do not share the same memory space, some kind of inter-process communication needs to be implemented, for example, using Python's native **multiprocessing** module. A more powerful but more complex solution is to use **Message Passing Interface (MPI)**.

IPython is particularly well-adapted to both solutions, and we will discuss them in this section. It provides a powerful and general architecture for parallel computing. Several IPython engines can run on different cores and/or different computers. Independent tasks can be easily and evenly distributed, thanks to **load balancing**. Data can be transferred from one engine to the other, making complex distributed algorithms possible from IPython.

Parallel computing is a particularly hard topic, and we will only cover the most basic aspects here.

Distributing tasks on multiple cores

The parallel computing features of IPython are extensive and highly customizable, but we will only show the simplest way of using them here. In addition, we will focus on the interactive usage of parallel computing, since that is the essence of IPython.

There are several steps to distribute code across multiple cores on one computer:

1. Launch several IPython engines (typically one per processor).
2. Create a `Client` object that acts as a proxy to these engines.
3. Use the client to launch tasks on the engines and retrieve the results.

Tasks can be launched synchronously or asynchronously:

1. With **synchronous** (or blocking) tasks, the client blocks right after the tasks have started, and returns the tasks' results when they have finished.
2. With **asynchronous** (non-blocking) tasks, the client returns an `ASyncResult` object immediately after the tasks have started. This object can be used to poll the task statuses asynchronously and to retrieve the results at any time after they have finished.

Starting the engines

The simplest way of starting the engines is to call in a system shell `ipcluster start` command. By default, this command will start one engine per core on the local machine. The number of engines can be specified with the `-n` option, for example, `ipcluster start -n 2` to start two engines. You can see the other available options with `ipcluster -h` and `ipcluster start -h`. In addition, the notebook has a panel named **Clusters** where you can launch and stop engines through a web interface.

Creating a Client instance

A client is used to send tasks to the engines. In an IPython console or in the notebook, we first need to import the Client class from the parallel subpackage.

```
In [1]: from IPython.parallel import Client
```

The next step is to create a Client instance.

```
In [2]: rc = Client()
```

IPython automatically detects the running engines. To check the number of running engines, we can do the following:

```
In [3]: rc.ids
Out[3]: [0, 1]
```

The ids attribute of the client gives the identifiers of the running engines. Here, there are two running engines on the local machine (it has a dual-core processing unit).

Using the parallel magic

The easiest way of sending tasks to the engines from IPython is to use the %px magic. It executes a single Python command on the engines.

```
In [4]: import os
In [5]: %px print(os.getpid())
[stdout:0] 6224
[stdout:1] 3736
```

By default, the command executes on all running engines and in synchronous mode. There are several ways to specify which engine(s) to target.

The first possibility is to use the %pxconfig magic command:

```
In [6]: %pxconfig --targets 1
In [7]: %px print(os.getpid())
3736
```

The --targets option accepts an index or a slice object, for example, ::2 for all engines with even indices. Here, we target only the second engine. All subsequent calls to %px will be executed on the specified targets.

An equivalent method is to use the %%px cell magic:

```
In [8]: %%px --targets :-1
        print(os.getpid())
[stdout:0] 6224
```

The options of `%%px` apply to the whole cell, which is particularly convenient in the notebook.

Another available option is the **blocking mode**. By default, the `%px` magic assumes a blocking mode. To enable the **non-blocking mode**, we can use the `--noblock` option.

```
In [9]: %%px --noblock
        import time
        time.sleep(1)
        os.getpid()
Out[9]: <AsyncResult: execute>
```

The task then executes asynchronously. The `%pxresult` magic command blocks the interpreter until the task has finished, and returns the result.

```
In [10]: %pxresult
Out[1:12]: 3736
```

Parallel map

The built-in `map` function applies a Python function to a sequence element-by-element. IPython provides a parallel `map` function, which is semantically equivalent, but dispatches the different tasks across the different engines. It is the simplest way to distribute tasks across multiple cores.

Creating a view

To use it, we first need to get a view to the engines, using the `Client` instance. A **view** represents one or several engines, and is obtained with an indexing syntax on the client. For example, to get a view on all engines, we use the following command:

```
In [11]: v = rc[:]
```

The view can then be used to launch tasks on the engines. Also, we can import packages on the engines with the `sync_imports()` method:

```
In [12]: with v.sync_imports():
             import time
importing time on engine(s)
```

Synchronous map

Let's define the following simple function:

```
In [13]: def f(x):
             time.sleep(1)
             return x * x
```

This function accepts a number and waits for one second before returning its square. To execute the function synchronously on all numbers between zero and nine, and using our two engines (so, using two CPUs), we can use the `v.map_sync()` method:

```
In [14]: v.map_sync(f, range(10))
Out[14]: [0, 1, 4, 9, 16, 25, 36, 49, 64, 81]
```

We obtain a list of results after a few seconds. Here, each engine has processed five tasks, for a total of 10 tasks:

```
In [15]: %timeit -n 1 -r 1 v.map_sync(f, range(10))
1 loops, best of 1: 5.02 s per loop
In [16]: %timeit -n 1 -r 1 map(f, range(10))
1 loops, best of 1: 10 s per loop
```

Asynchronous map

To execute the function asynchronously on the list of arguments, we can use the `v.map()` method:

```
In [17]: r = v.map(f, range(10))
In [18]: r.ready(), r.elapsed
Out[18]: False, 2.135
In [19]: r.get()
Out[19]: [0, 1, 4, 9, 16, 25, 36, 49, 64, 81]
In [20]: r.elapsed, r.serial_time
Out[20]: (5.023, 10.008)
```

The r variable is an `ASyncResult` object, with several attributes and methods that can be used to poll information about the progress, the elapsed time, and to get the tasks' results. The `elapsed` attribute returns, at any time, the elapsed time since the tasks began. The `serial_time` attribute is only available after the tasks have finished, and returns the cumulative time spent on all tasks across all engines. The `ready()` method returns, at any time, a value indicating whether the tasks have finished or not. The `get()` method blocks until the tasks have finished, and returns the results.

A practical example – Monte Carlo simulations

To illustrate the parallel computing possibilities offered by IPython, we will consider a new example. We want to estimate the Pi constant using *Monte Carlo simulations*. The principle is that if *n* points are randomly and uniformly sampled within a square of edge 1, the proportion of points that have a distance smaller than 1 from a fixed corner tends to *Pi/4*, if the number of points *n* tends to infinity. The following figure illustrates this fact:

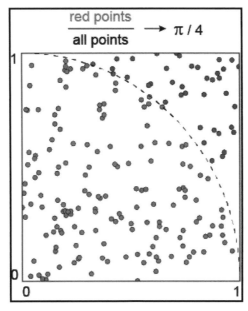

Estimation of Pi using a Monte-Carlo simulation

This is a particular example of a *Monte Carlo simulation*, which repeats a random experiment a large number of times, and takes an average at the end to estimate some quantity of interest that would be difficult to obtain with a deterministic method. Monte Carlo simulations are widespread in science, engineering, and finance. They are particularly convenient to parallelize, as it is generally a matter of executing the exact same function independently a large number of times.

Here, we will use this random experiment to estimate Pi. The precision obtained with this method is known to be low, and there are numerous methods that are far more efficient and precise. But, this example will be sufficient for introducing the parallel computing features of IPython.

First, we will write the Python code that executes the simulation. The `sample` function generates *n* points in the cube and returns the number of points that lie within the quarter disc.

```
In [1]: def sample(n):
            return (rand(n) ** 2 + rand(n) ** 2 <= 1).sum()
```

Since the *n*-long vector inside the parentheses is a mask array (that is, it contains Boolean values), its sum is the number of `True` values, that is, the number of points with an Euclidean distance from 0, smaller than 1.

Now, to estimate Pi, we just need to multiply `sample(n)` by `4/n`:

```
In [2]: n = 1000000.
In [3]: 4 * sample(n) / n
Out[3]: 3.142184
```

Since the real value of Pi is 3.1415926535..., we see that there are two correct digits (for this particular code execution) with one million points. We will now distribute this task on several cores. Assuming several engines have been started, for example, with `ipcluster start`, here is how we can parallelize the code:

```
In [4]: from IPython.parallel import Client
        rc = Client()
        v = rc[:]
        with v.sync_imports():
            from numpy.random import rand
In [5]: 4 * sum(v.map_sync(sample, [n] * len(v))) / (n * len(v))
Out[5]: 3.141353
```

Here, `len(v)` is the number of engines. We call the sample function `len(v)` times with the same argument n. The sum of all results is the total number of red points, and the total number of points is n * `len(v)`. Finally, we obtain the estimation of Pi with the same previous formula.

Using MPI with IPython

MPI is a famous standardized message passing system that is particularly efficient for parallel computing. We will assume that an MPI implementation is installed on your system (such as **Open-MPI**, `http://www.open-mpi.org`), as well as the **mpi4py** package for using MPI from Python (`http://mpi4py.scipy.org`). Information about how to install MPI can be found on these websites.

MPI on Windows

If you are on Windows, a possibility is to install Microsoft's MPI implementation available in the HPC Pack (http://www.microsoft.com/en-us/download/details.aspx?id=36045). Also, you may be interested in the Python Tools for Visual Studio (http://pytools.codeplex.com), which lets you turn Visual Studio into a Python IDE. It offers native support for IPython, and has been specifically designed for high-performance computing with MPI.

First, we need to create a specific IPython profile for MPI. Type in the following command in a shell:

```
ipython profile create --parallel --profile=mpi
```

Next, edit the file IPYTHONDIR/profile_mpi/ipcluster_config.py (IPYTHONDIR is generally ~/.ipython) and add the following line:

```
c.IPClusterEngines.engine_launcher_class = 'MPIEngineSetLauncher'
```

Now, to launch the cluster with four engines, type in the following command:

```
ipcluster start -n 4 --profile=mpi
```

To use MPI with IPython, we first need to write a function using MPI through mpi4py. In this example, we will compute the sum of all integers between 1 and 16 in parallel, across four cores. Let's write, in a file named psum.py, the following code:

```
from mpi4py import MPI
import numpy as np

# This function will be executed on all processes.
def psum(a):
    # "a" only contains a subset of all integers.
    # They are summed locally on this process.
    locsum = np.sum(a)

    # We allocate a variable that will contain the final result,
    that
# is the sum of all our integers.
    rcvBuf = np.array(0.0,'d')

    # We use a MPI reduce operation:
    #    * locsum is combined from all processes
    #    * these local sums are summed with the MPI.SUM operation
    #    * the result (total sum) is distributed back to all processes
    in
```

```
#     the rcvBuf variable
MPI.COMM_WORLD.Allreduce([locsum, MPI.DOUBLE],
    [rcvBuf, MPI.DOUBLE],
    op=MPI.SUM)
return rcvBuf
```

Finally, we can use this function interactively in IPython as follows:

```
In [1]: from IPython.parallel import Client

In [2]: c = Client(profile='mpi')

In [3]: view = c[:]

In [4]: view.activate() # enable magics

In [5]: view.run('psum.py') # the script is run on all processes

In [6]: view.scatter('a', np.arange(16)) # this array is scattered across processes

In [7]: %px totalsum = psum(a) # psum is executed on all processes
Parallel execution on engines: [0, 1, 2, 3]

In [8]: view['totalsum']

Out[8]: [120.0, 120.0, 120.0, 120.0]
```

More details about how to use MPI with IPython can be found on the following webpage from the official IPython documentation (where this example comes from):

```
http://ipython.org/ipython-doc/stable/parallel/parallel_mpi.html
```

Advanced parallel computing features of IPython

We covered only the very basics of the parallel computing features available in IPython. More advanced features include the following:

- Dynamic load balancing
- Pushing and pulling objects across engines
- Running engines on different computers, optionally using SSH tunnels
- Using IPython on an Amazon EC2 cluster with StarCluster
- Storing all requests and results in a database
- Managing task dependencies with a Directed Acyclic Graph (DAG)

These features are far beyond the scope of this book. Interested readers can find details about all those features in the official IPython documentation.

Using C in IPython with Cython

Distributing independent tasks across several cores is the easiest way to take advantage of the parallel capabilities of modern computers, thereby reducing the total execution time twofold or more. However, some algorithms cannot be easily split into independent subtasks. In addition, it may happen that the algorithm itself is far too slow in Python because it involves nested loops that cannot be vectorized. In this situation, a very interesting option could be to code a small but critical section of the code in C so as to considerably reduce the Python overhead. This solution does not involve any parallel computing feature, but it still allows to considerably improve the efficiency of a Python script. Additionally, nothing prevents using both techniques: partial C compilation and parallel computing with IPython.

The Cython package allows the compiling of a portion of the Python code without even converting it explicitly in C; it proposes an extended syntax in Python to call C functions and to define C types. The code in question is, then, automatically converted in C, compiled, and can then be used transparently from Python. In some situations when only pure Python code is possible, and when vectorization with NumPy is out of reach due to the particular nature of the algorithms, the speed improvement can be drastic and can reach several orders of magnitude.

In this section, we will see how to use Cython interactively in IPython. We will also look at an example of a pure Python function implementing a numerical algorithm, which can be compiled with Cython without too much effort for an execution more than 300 times faster.

Installing and configuring Cython

The Cython package is a bit more difficult to install than the other packages. The reason is that using Cython means compiling C code, which obviously requires a C compiler (for example the popular GNU C Compiler **gcc**). On Linux, gcc is already available or easily installable with the package manager, for example with `sudo apt-get install build-essential` on Ubuntu or Debian. On OS X, a possibility is to install Apple XCode. On Windows, you can install MinGW (`http://www.mingw.org`), which is an open-source distribution of gcc. Then, Cython can be installed as the other packages (see *Chapter 1*, *Getting started with IPython*). More information can be found at `http://wiki.cython.org/Installing`.

Configuring MinGW and Cython on Windows

On Windows, depending on the version of MinGW, error messages may appear when compiling Cython code. To fix this bug, you may need to open `C:\Python27\Lib\distutils\cygwinccompiler.py` (or a similar path depending on your specific configuration) and replace all occurrences of `-mno-cygwin` with `""` (empty string).

Also, make sure that `C:\MinGW\bin` is in the `PATH` environment variable. Finally, you may need to edit (or create) the file `C:\Python27\Lib\distutils\distutils.cfg` and add the following lines of code:

```
[build]
compiler = mingw32
```

You can find more information at `http://wiki.cython.org/InstallingOnWindows`.

Using Cython from IPython

With Cython, the code is generally written in a `.pyx` file, which is converted in C by Cython. Then, the resulting C program is compiled by the C compiler into a `.so` file (on Linux) or a `.pyd` file (on Windows), which can be normally imported in Python.

This process typically involves a `distutils setup.py` script which specifies the files to be compiled and also the different compiler options. Because this step is not particularly difficult, we will not cover it here. Rather, we will show how Cython can be easily used from IPython. The advantage is that the Cython and C compilations happen automatically under the hood and do not require a manual `setup.py` script. The IPython notebook is particularly useful here, as it is far more convenient to write multiline code in it than in the console.

Here we will show how to use the `%%cython` cell magic to execute Cython code from IPython. The first step is to load the `cythonmagic` extension.

```
In [1]: %load_ext cythonmagic
```

Then, the `%%cython` cell magic allows to write Cython code that will be automatically compiled. The functions defined in the cell become available in the interactive session, and can be used normally from Python.

```
In [2]: %%cython
        def square(x):
            return x * x
```

```
In [3]: square(10)
Out[3]: 100
```

Here, the call to `square(10)` involves the call to a compiled C function which computes the square of the number.

Accelerating a pure Python algorithm with Cython

Here, we will see how a pure Python algorithm involving nested loops can be converted in Cython for an interesting 10-fold speed improvement. This algorithm is the **Sieve of Eratosthenes**, a multi-millennial algorithm for finding all the prime integers less than a fixed number. This very classic algorithm consists of starting from all integers between 2 and *n*, and progressively removing the multiples of the prime numbers found so far. At the end of the algorithm, only the prime numbers remain. We will implement this algorithm in Python and show how it can be converted in Cython.

Pure Python version

The algorithm is a dozen-lines long in pure Python. This implementation could be improved and shortened in many ways (a one-liner algorithm exists!), but it will be sufficient for this example as we will mostly be interested in the *relative* execution times of the pure Python and Cython versions.

```
In [1]: def primes1(n):
            primes = [False, False] + [True] * (n - 2)
            i = 2
            # The exact code from here to the end of the function
            # will be referred as #SIEVE# in the next examples.
            while i < n:
                # we do not deal with composite numbers
                if not primes[i]:
                    i += 1
                    continue
                k = i * i
                # mark multiples of i as composite numbers
                while k < n:
                    primes[k] = False
                    k += i
                i += 1
            return [i for i in xrange(2, n) if primes[i]]
In [2]: primes(20)
Out[2]: [2, 3, 5, 7, 11, 13, 17, 19]
```

The `primes` variable contains Boolean values indicating whether the associated index is prime or not. We initialize it with only 0 and 1 being composite (non-prime), using the definition that a positive integer is prime if and only if it has exactly two positive divisors. Then, at each iteration over `i`, we will mark more and more numbers as composite numbers, without changing the prime ones. Every `i` represents a prime number, and the iteration over `k` allows to mark all multiples of `i` as composite numbers. At the end, we return the list of indices that are `True`, that is, all prime numbers less than `n`.

Now, let's take a look at the execution time of this function:

```
In [3]: n = 10000
In [4]: %timeit primes1(n)
100 loops, best of 3: 5.54 ms per loop
```

We will try to speed up this function using Cython.

Naïve Cython conversion

As a first attempt, we will simply use the exact same code in Cython.

```
In [5]: %load_ext cythonmagic
In [6]: %%cython
        def primes2(n):
            primes = [False, False] + [True] * (n - 2)
            i = 2
            #SIEVE#: see full code above
In [7]: timeit primes2(n)
100 loops, best of 3: 3.25 ms per loop
```

We achieve 70 percent speed improvement here just by adding `%%cython` at the top of the cell, but we can do much better by giving type information to Cython.

Adding C types

The speed improvement in the previous example was modest because the local variables are dynamically-typed Python variables. It means that the Python overhead due to its dynamic nature is still responsible for an important performance discrepancy as compared to pure C code. We can improve the performance by converting the Python variables into C variables with the `cdef` keyword.

```
In [8]: %%cython
        def primes3(int n):
            primes = [False, False] + [True] * (n - 2)
            cdef int i = 2
            cdef int k = 0
            #SIEVE#: see full code above
```

There are three changes compared to the naïve version: the n argument is statically declared as an integer, and the local variables i and k are now declared as C integer variables. The speed improvement is, then, much more interesting:

```
In [9]: timeit primes3(n)
1000 loops, best of 3: 538 us per loop
```

This function is now 10 times faster than the pure Python version, just by using the %%cython magic and a few type declarations. This result might even be improved with more adequate data structures.

In general, knowing the portion of the code that would be advantageously converted in Cython for a major speed improvement, requires some knowledge about the Python internals and, more importantly, requires performing extensive profiling. Python loops (especially nested loops), Python function calls, and high-level data structure manipulations inside tight loops are classical targets for Cython optimizations.

Using NumPy and Cython

In this section, we will show how to integrate NumPy arrays with Cython code. We will also see how calls to Python functions inside tight loops can be vastly optimized by converting the Python functions into C functions.

Python version

Here, we will use an example of a **stochastic process simulation**, namely a Brownian motion. This process describes the trajectory of a particle starting at x=0, and making random steps of +dx or -dx at each discrete time step, with dx being a small constant. This type of process appears frequently in finance, economy, physics, biology, and so on.

This specific process can be simulated very efficiently with NumPy's cumsum() and rand() functions. However, more complex processes may need to be simulated, for example, some models require instantaneous jumps when the position reaches a threshold. In these cases, vectorization is not an option and a manual loop is, therefore, unavoidable.

```
In [1]: def step():
            return sign(rand(1) - .5)

        def sim1(n):
            x = zeros(n)
            dx = 1./n
            for i in xrange(n - 1):
                x[i+1] = x[i] + dx * step()
            return x
```

The `step` function returns a random +1 or -1 value. It uses NumPy's `sign()` and `rand()` functions. In the `sim1()` function, the trajectory is first initialized as a NumPy vector with zeros. Then, at each iteration, a new random step is added to the trajectory. The `then` function returns the full trajectory. The following is an example of a trajectory:

```
In [2]: plot(sim1(10000))
```

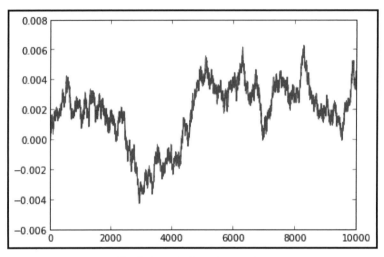

Simulation of a Brownian motion

Let's take a look to the execution time of this function.

```
In [3]: n = 10000
In [4]: timeit sim1(n)
1 loops, best of 3: 249 ms per loop
```

Cython version

For the Cython version, we will do two things. First, we will add C types for all local variables as well as for the NumPy array containing the trajectory. Also, we will convert the `step()` function to a pure C function that does not call any NumPy function. We will rather call pure C functions that are defined in the C standard library.

```
In [4]: %%cython
        import numpy as np
        cimport numpy as np
        DTYPE = np.double
        ctypedef np.double_t DTYPE_t
```

```
# We redefine step() as a pure C function, using only
# the C standard library.
from libc.stdlib cimport rand, RAND_MAX
from libc.math cimport round

cdef double step():
    return 2 * round(float(rand()) / RAND_MAX) - 1

def sim2(int n):
    # Local variables should be defined as C variables.
    cdef int i
    cdef double dx = 1. / n
    cdef np.ndarray[DTYPE_t, ndim=1] x = np.zeros(n,
dtype=DTYPE)
    for i in range(n - 1):
        x[i+1] = x[i] + dx * step()
    return x
```

We first need to import the standard NumPy library as well as a special C library, also called NumPy, which is part of the Cython package, with cimport. We define the NumPy dtype double and the corresponding C dtype double_t with ctypedef. It allows to define the exact type of the x array at compile-time rather than execution-time, resulting in major speed improvements. The number of dimensions of x is also specified inside the sim2() function. All local variables are defined as C variables with C types.

The step() function has been entirely rewritten. It is now a pure C function (defined with cdef). It uses the rand() function of the C standard library, which returns a random number between 0 and RAND_MAX. The round() function of the math library is also used to generate a random +1 or -1 value.

Let's check the execution time of the sim2() function:

In [5]: timeit sim2(n)

1000 loops, best of 3: 670 us per loop

The Cython version is 370 times faster than the Python version. The main reason for this dramatic speed improvement is that the Cython version uses only pure C code. All variables are C variables, and the calls to step, which previously required costly calls to a Python function, now only involve calls to a pure C function, thereby reducing considerably the Python overhead inside the loop.

More advanced options for accelerating Python code

Cython can also be used to interface existing C code or libraries with Python, but we won't cover this use case here.

Apart from Cython, there are other packages that accelerate Python code. `SciPy.weave` (http://www.scipy.org/Weave) is a SciPy subpackage that allows the inclusion of C/C++ code within Python code. **Numba** (http://numba.pydata.org/) uses just-in-time LLVM compilation to accelerate a pure Python code considerably by compiling it dynamically and transparently. It integrates nicely with NumPy arrays. Its installation requires llvmpy and meta.

Related projects include **Theano** (http://deeplearning.net/software/theano/), which allows to define, optimize, and evaluate mathematical expressions on arrays very efficiently by compiling them transparently on the CPU or on the graphics card. Similarly, **Numexpr** (https://code.google.com/p/numexpr/) can compile array expressions and take advantage of vectorized CPU instructions and multi-core processors.

Blaze (http://blaze.pydata.org/) is a project that is still in early development at the time of writing, and aims at combining all these dynamic compilation technologies together into a unified framework. It will also extend the notion of multidimensional array by allowing type and shape heterogeneity, missing values, labeled dimensions (such as in Pandas), and so on. Being developed by the creators of NumPy, it is likely to be a central project in the Python computing community in the near future.

Finally, **PyOpenCL** (http://mathema.tician.de/software/pyopencl) and **PyCUDA** (http://mathema.tician.de/software/pycuda) are Python wrappers to OpenCL and CUDA. These libraries implement C-like, low-level languages that can be compiled on modern graphics cards for taking advantage of their massively parallel architecture. Indeed, graphics cards contain hundreds of specialized cores that can process a function very efficiently on a large number of elements (**Single Instruction Multiple Data (SIMD)** paradigm). The speed improvement can be more than one order of magnitude faster compared to pure C code. **OpenCL** is an open standard language, whereas **CUDA** is a proprietary language owned by Nvidia Corporation. CUDA code runs on Nvidia cards only, whereas OpenCL is supported by most graphics cards as well as most CPUs. In the latter case, the same code is compiled on the CPU and takes advantage of multi-core processors and vectorized instructions.

Summary

In this chapter, we introduced two approaches to accelerate Python code: bypassing the Python overhead by converting the Python code into lower-level C code, or taking advantage of multi-core processors by distributing Python code across multiple computing units. Both approaches can even be used simultaneously. IPython considerably simplifies these techniques. Parallel computing and Cython can be used without IPython, but they require more boilerplate code.

In the next chapter, we will explore some advanced options to customize IPython.

6
Customizing IPython

IPython can be customized and extended for advanced uses. At the end of this chapter, you will know:

- How to create and use custom profiles
- How to use IPython extensions for advanced purposes
- How to use different languages in the notebook
- How to create your own extensions
- How to use rich representations in the frontend
- How to embed IPython in your Python code

IPython profiles

A profile is specific to a user on the local computer, and contains IPython preferences as well as the history, temporary and log files, and so on. By default, there is a single profile called the **default profile**. To create it manually, we can run the following command in the system shell:

```
ipython profile create
```

To specify a profile's name, we can use `ipython profile create name`.

Profile locations

Profiles are typically stored in ~/.ipython or ~/.config/ipython, where ~ is the current user's home directory. This directory is typically called the **IPython directory** and is sometimes referred to as IPYTHONDIR. To find the exact location of the profiles, we can run the ipython locate command for the IPython configuration directory, or ipython locate profile default for a specific profile directory, where default is the profile's name. A profile name is typically stored in a folder named profile_name within the IPython configuration folder.

By default, IPython starts with the default profile. To specify a different profile when running IPython, we can use the --profile command-line argument, for example:

```
ipython --profile=name
```

The IPython configuration files

In each profile, there is a special configuration file named ipython_config.py. This Python script is a placeholder for specifying various options. It contains a full template containing most possible options and it is fully documented, so that it should be straightforward to make changes.

For example, to enable the **pylab** mode automatically in a profile, as well as the qt event loop integration system, the following lines should appear in the corresponding ipython_config.py file:

```
# Enable GUI event loop integration ('qt', 'wx', 'gtk', 'glut',
# 'pyglet','osx').
c.InteractiveShellApp.gui = 'qt'

# Pre-load matplotlib and numpy for interactive use, selecting a
# particular matplotlib backend and loop integration.
c.InteractiveShellApp.pylab = 'qt'

# If true, an 'import *' is done from numpy and pylab, when using #
pylab
c.InteractiveShellApp.pylab_import_all = True
```

Loading scripts when IPython starts

You can have some Python scripts automatically loaded whenever IPython starts, just put them in `IPYTHONDIR/startup/`. This can be useful if you want to load modules or execute some scripts every time IPython starts.

IPython extensions

IPython extensions allow to implement entirely customized behaviors in IPython. They can be loaded manually with a simple magic command, or automatically when IPython starts.

Several extensions are natively included in IPython. They essentially allow to execute non-Python code from IPython. For example, the `cythonmagic` extension provides the `%%cython` cell magic for writing Cython code directly in IPython, as we saw in *Chapter 5*, *High Performance and Parallel Computing*. Similar built-in extensions include `octavemagic` and `rmagic` for executing Octave and R code in IPython. They are particularly useful in the notebook.

Third-party modules can also implement their own extensions, as we will see in this section with line-by-line profiling modules. Finally, we will show how to create new extensions.

Example – line-by-line profiling

The `line_profiler` and `memory_profiler` packages are line-by-line profilers that provide very precise details about the exact portions of the code that take too long or use too much memory. They provide magic commands that can be manually integrated with IPython. First, we need to install these packages, for example, using `easy_install`, `pip`, or Christoph Gohlke's web page for Windows users. The `psutil` package is required on Windows, and can be found on the same web page.

To activate the magic commands implemented in these two packages, we need to edit the IPython configuration file and add the following lines:

```
c.TerminalIPythonApp.extensions = [
    'line_profiler',
    'memory_profiler'
]
```

Then, the `lprun`, `mprun`, and `memit` magic commands are available. The line-by-line profilers work best when the function to profile is defined in a file rather than in the interactive session, because the profilers are then able to show the contents of each line in the profiling report.

As an example, let's create a script, `myscript.py`, using the following code:

```
import numpy as np
import matplotlib.pyplot as plt
def myfun():
    dx = np.random.randn(1000, 10000)
    x = np.sum(dx, axis=0)
    plt.hist(x, bins=np.linspace(-100, 100, 20))
```

This function simulates 10,000 random walks (Brownian motions) with 1,000 steps and plots a histogram of the particle position at the end of the simulation.

Now, we are going to load this function in IPython and profile it. The `%lprun` magic command accepts a Python statement as well as a list of functions to profile line by line, specified with a `-f` option:

```
In [1]: from myscript import myfun

In [2]: lprun -f myfun myfun()


    Timer unit: 5.13284e-07 s

    File: myscript.py
    Function: myfun at line 3
    Total time: 1.26848 s

    Line #       Hits           Time   Per Hit    % Time   Line Contents
    ==============================================================
       3                                                   def myfun():
       4          1        1783801 1783801.0      72.2       dx =
np.random.randn(1000, 1000)
       5          1         262352  262352.0      10.6       x =
np.cumsum(dx, axis=0)
       6          1         425142  425142.0      17.2       t =
np.arange(1000)
       7

np.histogram2d(t, x)
```

We can observe that most of the execution time happens in the creation of the `dx` array.

The `%mprun` magic command can be used similarly for memory profiling.

These line-by-line profilers are particularly useful when profiling complex Python applications. It is particularly convenient to do that interactively from IPython with those simple magic commands.

Creating new extensions

To create an extension, we need to create a Python module in a directory, which is in the Python path. A possibility is to put it in the current directory, or in IPYTHONDIR/extensions/.

An extension implements a load_ipython_extension(ipython) function, which takes the current InteractiveShell instance as an argument (and possibly unload_ipython_extension(ipython), which is called when the extension is unloaded). This instance can be used to register new magic commands, access the user namespace, execute code, and so on. This loading function is called when the extension is loaded, which happens when the %load_ext or %reload_ext magic command is executed. To automatically load a module when IPython starts, we need to add the module name to the c.TerminalIPythonApp.extensions list in the IPython configuration file.

The InteractiveShell instance

The InteractiveShell instance represents the active IPython interpreter. Useful methods and attributes include register_magics(), to create new magic commands, and user_ns, to access the user namespace. You can explore all the instance's attributes interactively from IPython with tab completion. For that, you need to execute the following command to get the current instance:

```
ip = get_ipython()
```

Example – executing C++ code in IPython

In this example, we will create a new extension to execute C++ code directly from IPython. This is only a pedagogical example, and in a real-world project, it might be a better idea to use Cython or SciPy.weave.

The extension defines a new cell magic named cpp. The idea is that one will be able to write C++ code directly in the cell, and it will be automatically compiled and executed. The cell output will contain the standard output of the code. Here is an explanation of how this extension works:

- We create a new class derived from IPython.core.magic.Magics

- In this class, we create a new method with a cell_magic decorator: it will implement the cpp cell magic

- This method accepts the cell's code as input, writes this C++ code in a temporary file, and calls the g++ compiler to create an executable

- The method then calls the newly created executable and returns the output
- In the `load_ipython_extension` function, we register this magic class

The following code should be written in a `cppmagic.py` script:

```
import IPython.core.magic as ipym

@ipym.magics_class
class CppMagics(ipym.Magics):
    @ipym.cell_magic
    def cpp(self, line, cell=None):
        """Compile, execute C++ code, and return the standard
output."""
        # Define the source and executable filenames.
        source_filename = 'temp.cpp'
        program_filename = 'temp.exe'
        # Write the code contained in the cell to the C++ file.
        with open(source_filename, 'w') as f:
            f.write(cell)
        # Compile the C++ code into an executable.
        compile = self.shell.getoutput("g++ {0:s} -o {1:s}".format(
            source_filename, program_filename))
        # Execute the executable and return the output.
        output = self.shell.getoutput(program_filename)
        return output

def load_ipython_extension(ipython):
    ipython.register_magics(CppMagics)
```

The following screenshot shows how this extension can be conveniently used to write C++ code in the IPython notebook:

```
In [1]:  %load_ext cppmagic

In [2]:  %%cpp
         #include<iostream>
         int main()
         {
             std::cout << "Hello world!";
         }

Out[2]:   ['Hello world!']
```

Executing C++ code in the IPython notebook

This code works on Windows and can be easily adapted to Unix systems.

Improving this example

This example could be improved in many ways: temporary files could have unique names and could be stored in a special temporary directory, compilation errors could be nicely handled and redirected to IPython, and so on. The interested reader can take a look at the built-in Cython, Octave, and R magic extensions in IPython/extensions/ that are somewhat similar to this example. More generally, the same techniques can be used to run non-Python code in IPython. It may even be possible to share variables between Python and the other languages.

The IPython extensions are particularly powerful in the context of the notebook, because they notably allow the implementation of arbitrarily complex behaviors to the cells' code.

Extensions index

An index of IPython extensions created by IPython users can be found at https://github.com/ipython/ipython/wiki/Extensions-Index. If you have developed your own extension, do not hesitate to add it here!

Rich representations in the frontend

The notebook and the Qt console can display richer representations of objects. Both can display bitmap and SVG images, and the notebook also supports videos, HTML code, and mathematical equations in LaTeX. It is particularly easy to display rich objects with classes: one just needs to implement a method called _repr_*_ with * being svg, png, jpeg, html, json, pretty, or latex. For instance, let's define a class, Disc, with a SVG representation method:

```
In [1]: class Disc(object):

          def __init__(self, size, color= ared'):

              self.size = size
              self.color = color


          def _repr_svg_(self):

              return """<svg xmlns="http://www.w3.org/2000/svg"
version="1.1">

                      <circle cx="{0:d}" cy="{0:d}" r="{0:d}"
fill="{1:s}" />

                      </svg>""".format(self.size, self.color)
```

The constructor of this class accepts a radius size in pixels and a color as a string. Then, when an instance of this class is directed on the standard output, the SVG representation is automatically shown in the cell's output as shown in the following screenshot:

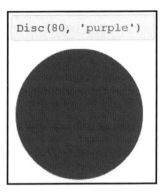

SVG representation in the IPython notebook

Another way of displaying rich representations of objects is to use the `IPython.display` module. You can interactively obtain the list of all supported representations with tab completion. For example, the following screenshot shows how LaTeX equations can be rendered in the notebook:

```
In [1]:  import IPython.display as dsp

In [2]:  dsp.Math(r"\sum_{n=1}^\infty \frac{1}{n^2} = \frac{\pi^2}{6}")
```

Out[2]: $$\sum_{n=1}^{\infty} \frac{1}{n^2} = \frac{\pi^2}{6}$$

LaTeX equations in the IPython notebook

The rich display features of the notebook make it particularly adapted to the creation of pedagogical contents, presentations, blog posts, books, and so on, as notebooks can be exported in formats such as HTML or PDF.

Yet richer interactive representations will probably be possible in a future version of IPython with the support of custom JavaScript extensions and widgets in the notebook.

Embedding IPython

It is possible to launch IPython from any Python script, even when the standard Python interpreter runs the script. It can be useful in some occasions when you need to interact with a complex Python program at some point, and where using the IPython interpreter for the whole program is not possible or unwanted. For example, in a scientific computing context, you may want to pause the program after some automatic, computationally-intensive algorithms to look at the data, draw some plots, and so on, before resuming the program. Another possible use case is the integration of a widget in a graphical user interface to let the user interact with the Python environment through the IPython command-line interface.

The easiest way to integrate IPython in a program is to call `IPython.embed()` at any point in your Python program (after `import IPython`). You can also specify custom options, including the input/output templates in the command-line interface, the startup/exit messages, and so on. You can find more information at `http://ipython.org/ipython-doc/stable/interactive/reference.html#embedding-ipython`.

Final words

At this point, you should be convinced about the great power and flexibility of IPython. Not only does IPython natively offer an impressive number of useful features, it also lets you extend and customize it in virtually any aspect. It should be noted, however, that this project is still evolving. Although it was created more than 10 years ago, Version 1.0 has still not been released at the time of writing. The core features of IPython are now quite stable and mature. The notebook, which is the most recent feature, is expected to evolve importantly in the coming years. The possibility to create custom interactive widgets in the notebook is planned and is likely to be a major feature of the whole project. More information about the upcoming developments can be found at `https://github.com/ipython/ipython/wiki/Roadmap:-IPython` and `http://ipython.org/_static/sloangrant/sloan-grant.html`.

Finally, IPython is an active open source project, meaning that anyone is welcome to contribute. Contributing can be as simple as reporting or fixing a bug, but it is always highly useful and greatly appreciated! Relatedly, anyone is welcome to request some help online, in respect of the common etiquette rules, of course. The developers and the most active users are always willing to help. Here are some useful links:

- GitHub project page: `https://github.com/ipython/ipython`
- Wiki: `https://github.com/ipython/ipython/wiki`
- User mailing list: `http://mail.scipy.org/mailman/listinfo/ipython-user`
- Chat room: `https://www.hipchat.com/ghSp7E1uY`

Summary

In this chapter we described how IPython can be customized and extended, notably through extensions. Non-Python languages can also be called from IPython, which is particularly convenient in the notebook where any code can be copied and pasted in a cell and transparently compiled and evaluated in the current Python namespace. The notebook also supports rich display features and, soon, interactive widgets, making it the most advanced tool to date for interactive programming and computing in Python.

Index

S

T

U

V

W

Thank you for buying
Learning IPython for Interactive
Computing and Data Visualization

About Packt Publishing

Packt, pronounced 'packed', published its first book "*Mastering phpMyAdmin for Effective MySQL Management*" in April 2004 and subsequently continued to specialize in publishing highly focused books on specific technologies and solutions.

Our books and publications share the experiences of your fellow IT professionals in adapting and customizing today's systems, applications, and frameworks. Our solution based books give you the knowledge and power to customize the software and technologies you're using to get the job done. Packt books are more specific and less general than the IT books you have seen in the past. Our unique business model allows us to bring you more focused information, giving you more of what you need to know, and less of what you don't.

Packt is a modern, yet unique publishing company, which focuses on producing quality, cutting-edge books for communities of developers, administrators, and newbies alike. For more information, please visit our website: www.packtpub.com.

About Packt Open Source

In 2010, Packt launched two new brands, Packt Open Source and Packt Enterprise, in order to continue its focus on specialization. This book is part of the Packt Open Source brand, home to books published on software built around Open Source licences, and offering information to anybody from advanced developers to budding web designers. The Open Source brand also runs Packt's Open Source Royalty Scheme, by which Packt gives a royalty to each Open Source project about whose software a book is sold.

Writing for Packt

We welcome all inquiries from people who are interested in authoring. Book proposals should be sent to author@packtpub.com. If your book idea is still at an early stage and you would like to discuss it first before writing a formal book proposal, contact us; one of our commissioning editors will get in touch with you.

We're not just looking for published authors; if you have strong technical skills but no writing experience, our experienced editors can help you develop a writing career, or simply get some additional reward for your expertise.

Spring Python 1.1

ISBN: 978-1-84951-066-0   Paperback: 264 pages

Create powerful and versatile Spring Python applications using pragmatic libraries and useful abstractions

1. Maximize the use of Spring features in Python and develop impressive Spring Python applications

2. Explore the versatility of Spring Python by integrating it with frameworks, libraries, and tools

3. Discover the non-intrusive Spring way of wiring together Python components

4. Packed with hands-on-examples, case studies, and clear explanations for better understanding

Python Geospatial Development

ISBN: 978-1-84951-154-4   Paperback: 508 pages

Build a complete and sophisticated mapping application from scratch using Python tools for GIS development

1. Build applications for GIS development using Python

2. Analyze and visualize Geo-Spatial data

3. Comprehensive coverage of key GIS concepts

4. Recommended best practices for storing spatial data in a database

5. Draw maps, place data points onto a map, and interact with maps

Please check **www.PacktPub.com** for information on our titles

Python Text Processing with NLTK 2.0 Cookbook

ISBN: 978-1-84951-360-9   Paperback: 272 pages

Over 80 practical recipes for using Python's NLTK suite of libraries to maximize your Natural Language Processing capabilities

1. Quickly get to grips with Natural Language Processing – with Text Analysis, Text Mining, and beyond

2. Learn how machines and crawlers interpret and process natural languages

3. Easily work with huge amounts of data and learn how to handle distributed processing

4. Part of Packt's Cookbook series: Each recipe is a carefully organized sequence of instructions to complete the task as efficiently as possible

Instant Django 1.5 Application Development Starter [Instant]

ISBN: 978-1-78216-356-5   Paperback: 78 pages

Jump into Django with this hands-on guide to practical web application development with Python

1. Learn something new in an Instant!
A short, fast, focused guide delivering immediate results.

2. Work with the database API to create a data-driven app

3. Learn Django by creating a practical web application

4. Get started with Django's powerful and flexible template system

Please check **www.PacktPub.com** for information on our titles